TOMORROW'S WORLD

THE RISE OF THE ROBOTS

THE RISE OF THE ROBOTS

Written by
Madeline Tyler

Illustrated by
Martyn Cain

First published in 2026 by Hungry Tomato Ltd, F15, Old Bakery Studios, Blewetts Wharf, Malpas Road, Truro, Cornwall, TR1 1QH, UK.

Editor: Millie Burdett
Graphic Designer: Amy Orris
Cover Designers: Amy Harvey and Sam Fleetwood
Consultant: Zhou Xiaohu

With thanks to Nicola Carthy

A CIP catalog record for this book is available from the British Library.

Information in this book is up to date as of the time of writing.

ISBN: 9781835694626 (soft cover)
ISBN: 9781835694800 (hard cover)

Printed and bound in China

Discover more at
www.hungrytomato.com

MIX
Paper | Supporting responsible forestry
FSC® C158492

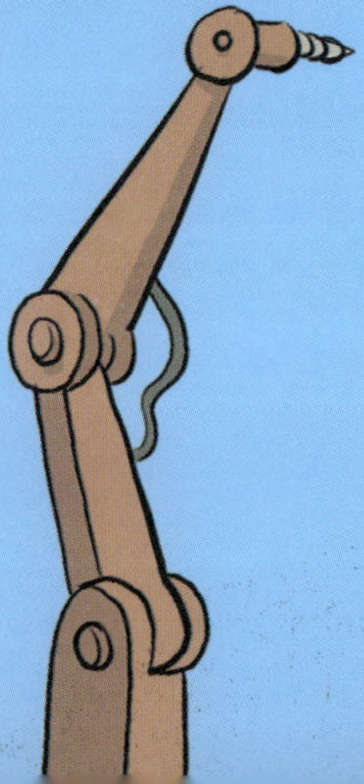

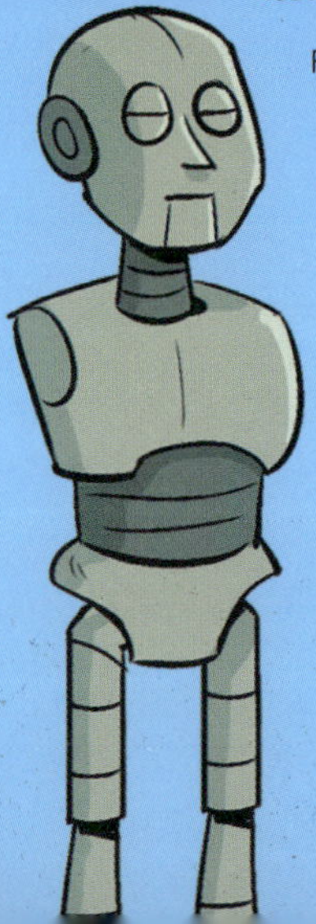

CONTENTS

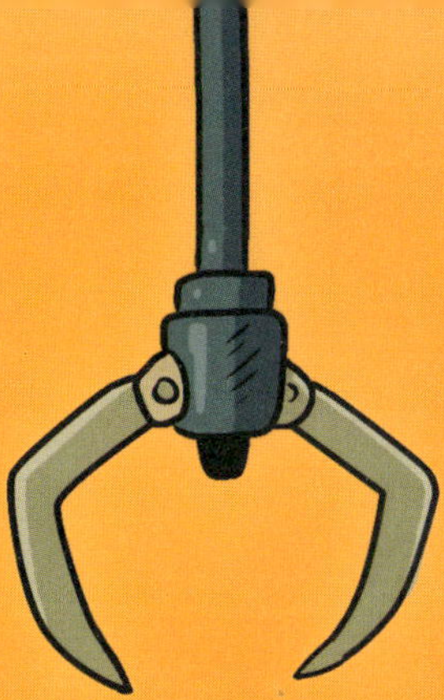 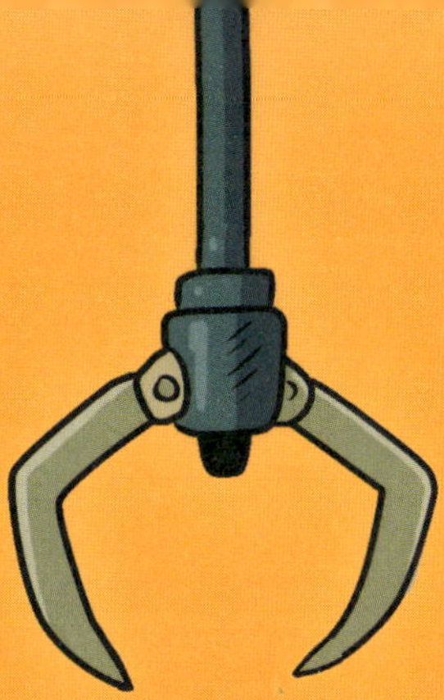

Chapter 1

WE'RE LIVING IN A ROBOT WORLD

I'm a human. You're a human. Humans are pretty great, wouldn't you agree? Some humans are small, some are tall, some are strong, some are brave, some are clever, and some are quick.

In fact, some humans are so strong and so brave and so quick that they might seem...

SUPERHUMAN!

Human beings are super in lots of ways but, even though it might not always seem like it, no matter how strong, smart, or speedy they are, they are all still human. Yes, even you!

Sometimes there are places on Earth and in outer space where it would be too difficult or too dangerous to send a person – even the very, very bravest of humans.

Can you imagine sending a human on a one-way trip to the edge of our solar system?! Astronauts might one day be able to fly a rocket to Saturn, and maybe one day there will even be people walking on the surface of Mars... but not yet!

Some jobs are too difficult, too dangerous, too fiddly, or too scary, but some jobs are just too boring! Human beings are very clever and very busy, so sometimes it would be much easier if something else could do these jobs for us so we can focus on the more important things! You know, things like teaching a group of squirrels how to play piano, training to become the world's first professional hide-and-seek champion, or trying to break the world record for the most blueberries balanced on one elbow!

SO, WHAT CAN WE DO? AND WHO CAN DO ALL OF THESE JOBS INSTEAD OF US?

Human beings have achieved incredible things, but we can achieve even greater things when we work as a team. Scientists from around the world have been working together to build machines that can help us at home, in space, and even at the bottom of the ocean!

ENTER THE ROBOTS.

Is it a bird? Is it a plane?
No! It's a team of super-fast, super-strong, and super-brave robots heading our way!

Yes, that's right. Robots are no longer just a fantasy. They might once have only existed in books and movies, but now robots are really part of our lives and they're here to save the world...

WHAT DO *YOU* THINK A ROBOT IS?

Are you imagining a massive metal monster shooting lasers out of its eyes? Or maybe a terrifically terrifying team of super-scary bots, flying down from a giant spaceship ready to take over the world? If you are, it sounds like we might need to s l o w it down and go back to basics.

WHAT IS A ROBOT?

A robot is a machine that can be controlled by a computer and can work on its own to follow instructions.

Robots are incredible and very, very powerful, but don't worry – they won't be taking over the world anytime soon. They've been created to give us a helping hand (or claw!), not to end the world!

Just like people, robots come in lots of different shapes and sizes. Although they're all pretty similar on the inside, on the outside they can look veeeeery different. Some robots look like people, and some robots really don't (unless you know anyone who looks like this!).

OK, GOT IT! SO, HOW DO YOU SPOT A ROBOT?

Do you think robots have taken over your town? Do you suspect your teacher might be a robot? Let's look at the basic traits.

WHEN LOOKING FOR ROBOTS, LOOK OUT FOR THESE SIGNS:

- [ ] Some kind of body that can move
- [ ] Sensors (these might look like small cameras, tiny lightbulbs, or mini microphones)
- [ ] Something to give them power, like a battery
- [ ] A computer that tells them what to do

Robots have computers inside them and these computers work a bit like your **HUGE MASSIVE BRAIN**. The computer controls all the bits of the robot and makes sure it can do all of the things it needs to do.

A robot can then be given instructions called a computer program and can sometimes be left to do its job all on its own. Clever robot!

The computer program might tell the robot to pick things up from a conveyor belt and put them down somewhere else, or it might tell the robot how to do something far more exciting, like walk around or even dance! And some can even talk!

TRY THIS:
Let's put this to the test. Take 5 steps. Stop. Scratch your head. Stop. Look around. Stop. Wave. Stop. Say "Hello!". These instructions are a bit like a program that could be given to a robot.

Robots might look like they come from the future, but they have actually been around longer than you might think.

LET'S TRAVEL BACK IN TIME...

The first modern robot was a happy little guy called Unimate. Unimate was made all the way back in the 1950s. Unimate probably doesn't look like what you imagine when you hear the word "robot", but it was a very important part of robot history.

Unimate was a robotic arm, and was the first ever robot to work in a factory. It paved the way for future industrial robots and was so important that it's now part of the Robot Hall of Fame at Carnegie Mellon University, USA.

ROBOT TYPES...

Believe it or not, people had been designing robots for hundreds of years before Unimate was created. It's because of these early robots that we have the mind-blowing, life-saving robots of today!

There are SO MANY different types of robots. It can be easier to think about them when they're sorted into different groups.

Robots are grouped based on what they look like or what their jobs are:

HUMANOIDS

Humanoid robots, or androids, look like us!

DRONES

Drones are flying robots. Whoooooooosh!

MICROROBOTS

Microrobots and nanorobots are teeny-tiny, itty-bitty, microscopic baby bots.

INDUSTRIAL ROBOTS

Industrial robots are used in factories to help us make and build things.

SPACE ROBOTS

Can you guess where we might find space robots? That's right – up in space!

MEDICAL ROBOTS

Medical robots work in hospitals, helping doctors to perform operations and doing other tasks that help make us better.

AUTONOMOUS

Autonomous vehicles are robotic cars, boats, and planes – they can drive on their own without a human!

So, you're here to meet some robots, are you? Well then, what you are waiting for? Let's get started! Stop reading this sentence, there's more info about these robots further down the page!

HUMANOIDS / ANDROIDS

These robots are designed and built to look like you and me. Well, not *exactly* like you and me. They might not have soft, squidgy bodies or ten fingers and ten toes, but they do have:

- A human-shaped head
- A human-shaped body
- Two arms
- Two legs

Androids are becoming more and more lifelike, and it's becoming more difficult to tell them apart from real humans.

NOW TELL ME THIS. HAVE YOU EVER THOUGHT THAT ROBOTS COULD BE BEAUTIFUL? WHAT ABOUT GRACEFUL?

DANCING BOTS

At China's Spring Gala Festival in 2025, sixteen androids stole the show with their impressive dance moves! The robots walked onto the stage dressed up in flowery padded jackets (fancy!) and danced alongside sixteen human dancers. They bopped and boogied, shook their hips, and twirled their handkerchiefs just like the human dancers!

Androids are the perfect robots for working alongside humans because they can move similarly to how we do! They're not big or bulky or clunky – making them the perfect dance partners.

SPORTY BOTS

Androids are great at playing sports, too. Some clever scientists have created humanoid robots that can play table tennis with each other. Not with the scientists – with each other! These sporty bots can hit the ball back and forth, and back and forth, and back and forth, and... you get the picture.

Some scientists believe that humanoid robots – robots that look like us, move like us, and maybe even one day talk like us, act like us, and feel emotions like we do – could be the future of robotics. In fact, incredibly lifelike androids might not be too far away...

MEET SOPHIA!

Sophia is an android who doesn't look much like a robot at all, as long as you don't look too closely! She can make 62 different expressions with her face and have a chat with you about the weather. Talking about the weather might sound boring, but not many robots can do this, and that makes Sophia very exciting! In 2017, Sophia became the first ever robot to be given a passport and become an actual citizen of a country.

None of this means that Sophia is a person, but as robots become more and more like humans, it's important that we know what makes a person a person and what makes a robot a robot.

DRONES

Drones are remote-controlled flying robots. When they fly, they can sometimes make a buzzzzzzzing sound, a bit like a swarm of bees. But don't worry, these flying robots don't sting!

They can be controlled by someone on the ground using a remote control, like a big, fancy toy, or scientists can program them with a set of instructions so the drones can move automatically – whether that's forward, backward, up, down, left, right, or round and round in circles. Don't get dizzy!

Some of these instructions can be very complicated. When drones are fitted with multicolored, flashing lights, these instructions can be used to make hundreds and even THOUSANDS of drones all fly together and arrange themselves to make pictures in the sky.

BEAUTIFUL DRONES

For China's National Day celebrations in 2024, more than 10,000 drones were launched to light up the night sky. They flew together to create incredible images, including a "cyber firework"! This display was SO IMPRESSIVE that it broke two Guinness World Records!

Who knew robots could be so pretty and so creative?!

TINY BOTS

If you're wondering what these teeny tiny little bugs are doing in a book about robots, well, you're in for a surprise! Before you try to squish them, these mini machines are actually robots!

FUN FACT: NANOMETERS

Microrobots and nanorobots are very small but very useful little bots. Microrobots are robots that are smaller than 1 millimeter (0.04 inches). Nanorobots are even smaller – they're measured in something called nanometers

WHAT'S A NANOMETER?

Well, imagine the smallest, teeniest, tiniest, most miniscule thing you can. Now, imagine that this teeny tiny thing has been made even smaller. Even smaller! A nanometer is even smaller than that!

Get ready for some seriously tiny science! If you thought 1 millimeter was small, there are 1,000,000 nanometers in 1 millimeter. Yes, ONE MILLION! Don't worry if you can't imagine something that tiny – not many people can!

ROBOTIC DOCTORS

Microrobots and nanorobots are still very new, but scientists think they could one day be sent inside our bodies to reach the places doctors can't see. Maybe these tiny little robotic doctors will one day save the world!

Robots can be found pretty much everywhere! From industrial robots in factories to medical robots in hospitals, scientists from across the scientific world are working together to build robots that can make our lives much easier.

Robots are used by lots of different people, not just scientists and robot-experts. In fact, robots are becoming so easy to use that you could probably come across robots in people's kitchens, living rooms, and even their garages. That's right – robotic cars are real! Fancy a drive?

WHAT IS THE STUDY OF ROBOTS CALLED?

Robotics is the study of robots. It's all about designing, building, and using them. From androids to drones to nanorobots and microrobots and some robots we haven't met yet, robotics covers them all!

Robotics covers A LOT of different, complicated things – when we talk about robotics, we might be talking about designing a robot's legs, writing computer programs to make a robot dance, or a million other things!

To make things a bit simpler, scientists sometimes break robotics down into smaller, bite-size groups so the right people are always working on the right bits.

BREAKING IT DOWN:

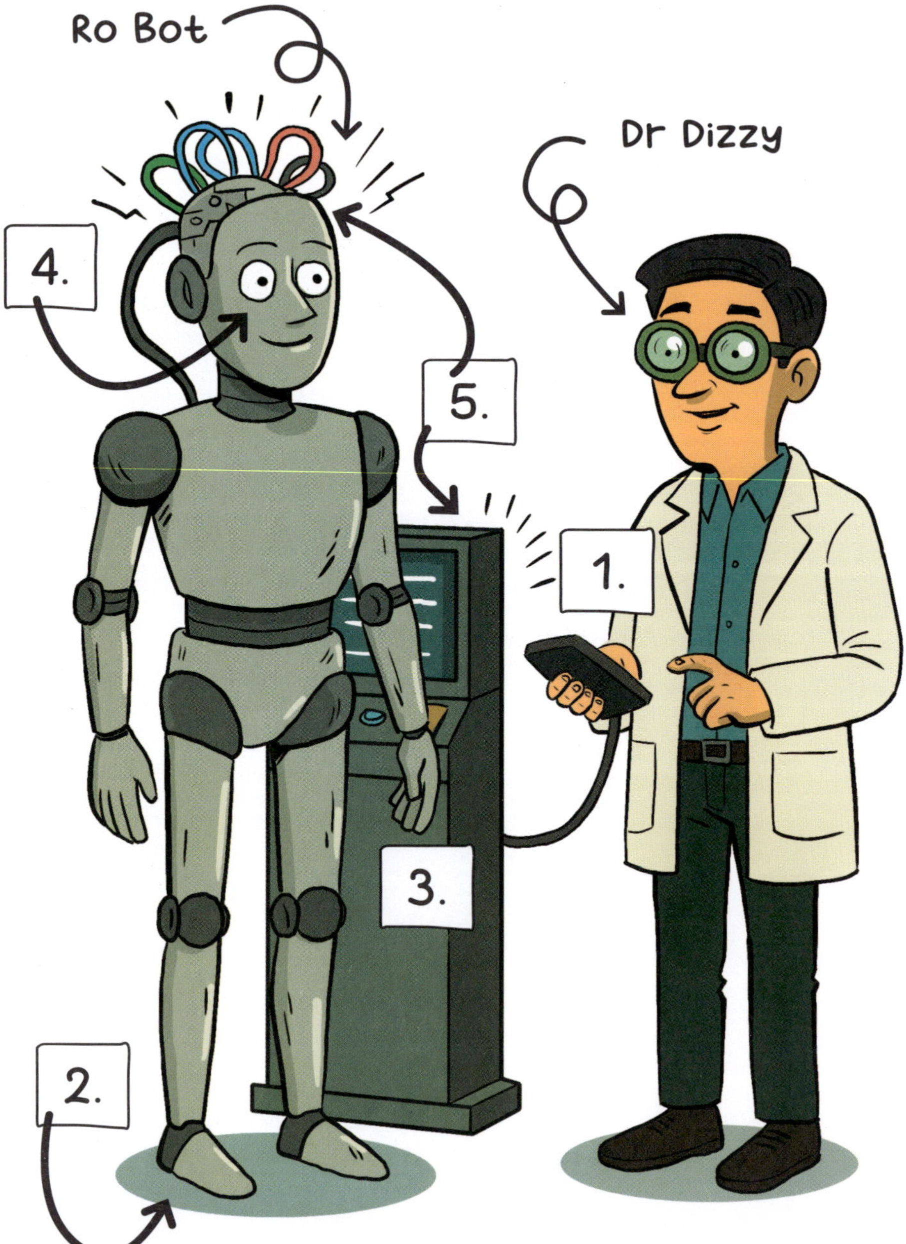

1. HOW WE TALK TO ROBOTS

The Human Robot Interface (or HRI for short) is how people can talk to robots and give them the instructions they need to do their jobs.

2. HOW ROBOTS MOVE

This is sometimes called mobility or locomotion. Does the robot use two legs or four? Does it have wheels? Or maybe it flies?

3. THE PARTS OF A ROBOT

Robots sometimes need to pick things up or push things around. The arms, pincers, claws, pushers, or hands a robot might use are called manipulators and end-effectors (more on this later).

4. HOW A ROBOT SEES THE WORLD

Robots use sensors to take in information about the world. These sensors tell the robot of any obstacles that might be in their way. Watch out, Ro Bot!

5. HOW A ROBOT UNDERSTANDS THE WORLD

Computer programs are written in special computer languages so robots can understand what we're asking them to do. The people who write these programs are called programmers or computer scientists.

WHO STUDIES ROBOTICS?

Scientists who study, design, and build robots are called roboticists and they are very clever indeed! Some roboticists design and build the inside bits of a robot, some work on the outside bits, and some study how we can use robots. Robots are **very** complicated to build. Roboticists might come from different backgrounds, all around the world, but they work together because they love robots and want to build the best ones they can.

ROBOTICISTS WHO ARE CREATING THE MACHINES OF THE FUTURE:

MECHANICAL ENGINEERS:

"I design and build the bits of a robot that you can see and the bits that move around, like the arms and motors!"

COMPUTER SCIENTISTS:

"I'm a computer scientist! You might have guessed that I create the computer programs that control the robots."

Robots really are everywhere. Roboticists are working closely with other scientists all the time to see how robots can be used in other areas of science and in every part of our lives.

Robots in space? Robots under the sea? Robots in our homes, in our factories, in our schools, and in our hospitals? Roboticists are on the case to create handy little (and big!) helpers that we can work with to solve problems of the present and future, on Earth and beyond! So, how do they do it?

Chapter 2

HOW TO BUILD A BOT

BUILDING A ROBOT ISN'T EASY. LOOK AT ALL THOSE WIRES AND BOLTS AND BUTTONS. HOW DO WE KNOW WHICH PARTS GO WHERE?

The roboticists who design robots have to think very carefully about how to create the best robot for the job. Designing the wrong kind of robot could end in disaster!

Some robots need wheels, some need hands, some need wings to let them fly, and some need friendly faces that make us feel all warm and fuzzy. If a robot has the wrong parts, it might not be able to do its job properly. Does a robot need a claw or a pusher? Does it need to be as light as a feather or a strong, heavy BIG BOT? These are all things a roboticist needs to think about!

Building a robot, even the ones that don't look like people, is a bit like building a human. Don't believe me? Let's take a look! What would a checklist for building a human look like...

BUILDING A HUMAN

YOU WOULD NEED:

- A body for your human
- A way to make your human move (think legs and muscles!)
- Arms and hands (or, a way to make your human pick things up)
- Senses (how else would your human know where they are?!)
- A source of power
- A big brain!
- A way to talk to your human (do you write your instructions down, do you say them out loud, or is your human remote-controlled?!)

Now we've built a human,

LET'S BUILD A ROBOT!

YOU WOULD NEED:

- A body for your robot
- A way to make your robot move (actuators are the "muscles" of a robot – they're the things that make it GO!)
- Manipulators and end-effectors (ways that your robot can pick things up or move things about)
- Sensors (ways for your robot to "see" the world and know where they are)
- A source of power (maybe a big battery)
- A computer that tells them what to do
- A way to talk to your robot

STEP ONE: CHOOSE A BODY!

The first step in building any robot is choosing its body. Will it be big, small, square, round, soft, or rigid? Do you need your robot to be heavy or light, fast or slow?

The body of a robot is very important because it's the bit that all the other parts are connected to. Just take a look at yourself! Your arms and legs and even your head are all connected to your body, so if you had no body, you'd have nothing else either!

Android bodies look very similar to human bodies, but there are plenty of other bodies on offer for a whole variety of robot needs.

ROOMBA

Roomba is a type of robotic vacuum cleaner. It zips and buzzes across the ground cleaning up your messes. A big old human body would make it difficult for Roomba to move quickly and fit into tight spaces. Instead, Roomba is round and cylindrical, a bit like a flat, squished ball.

Roomba can move around tight corners, under furniture, and dodge any little furry friends who might be in its way...

MODULAR ROBOT

Some robot bodies are actually made up of lots of smaller bodies. In 2019, some super-brainy scientists at Massachusetts Institute of Technology (MIT) in the USA built modular robots. These robots are made up of lots of little robotic cubes called modules.

These clever cubes can roll around, leap through the air, and climb over and around each other. When they need to be ONE BIG ROBOT rather than lots of little robots, all the mini modules join together.

STEP TWO: MAKE IT MOVE!

Great! Now your robot has a body, you need to give it the parts to make it move! Staying still is boring, so let's give your robot some legs, wheels, tracks, or maybe even some wings, and get this robot on the go.

Mobility and locomotion are different words that mean "moving". Some roboticists specialize in mobility and locomotion.

No, this doesn't mean they move around a lot. It's their job to study different ways of getting around and how we can build robots that move faster, slower, smoother, or more efficiently.

WHAT BODY PARTS ARE NEEDED?

Different places need different movements, and different movements need different body parts.

We use our legs and feet to get around all the time, but can you imagine trying to make your way through water without being able to kick your legs or flap your arms?

Not easy! Maybe even impossible!

Now, let's not get too carried away.
If you need a robot to go underwater, then you'll need to make sure it can swim. Unless you plan on sending your poor little robot on a one-way mission to the bottom of the ocean, wheels won't be much good, and neither would tiny little legs.

Roboticists think about all of these things and figure out whether a robot needs wings, tracks, legs (and how many!), wheels, or something else! No matter how a robot is getting around, it needs an actuator. This is the thing that gives it the FORCE to make it GO!

MOVING AS A ROBOT

Robots can use their actuators to run, walk, roll, shuffle, wheel, fly, slither, and swim. They can dance, jump, hover, float, and glide. Not **all** robots can do **all** of these things.

Robots with legs are great at climbing steps, crossing w i d e gaps, or walking across rough ground. But what's better: two legs or four? Or maybe more? Six? Eight?

That guy has got a lot of legs, is that really necessary?

MOVING AS A HUMAN

When we need to move across different surfaces, we might change into different shoes. Snow boots and skis can help us trudge and glide through snow without slipping across the ice. Special boots can make it easy to walk across mud – these boots might make you feel like you have tracks on your feet, like a big, strong tank.

STEP THREE: PINCERS OR CLAWS?

We use robots to help us with lots of different things. Sometimes we need them to pick things up very, very delicately. Sometimes we need them to lift huge, heavy things that would be far too heavy for a tiny little human to carry. Sometimes we need them to push things around. And sometimes we need them to fix things.

Robots need things like arms and hands that can let them do all of these jobs. We call these parts manipulators and end-effectors.

Humans can't change their hands for different ones every time they need to do a different job. Instead, when we want to play tennis, we pick up a racket, or when we need to do some DIY, we might pick up a hammer or a spanner.

WHAT ARE MANIPULATORS?

Manipulators are like our arms. They have rigid parts that are connected by joints that can bend and move.

WHAT ARE END-EFFECTORS?

End-effectors are like our hands. They're attached to the ends of manipulators.

Roboticists usually design robots to do one job and do it very, very well. Instead of arms and hands, robots sometimes have manipulators and end-effectors that are designed especially to do specific jobs. So, instead of needing to pick tools up with their hands, the tools *are* their hands!

DO YOU NEED YOUR ROBOT TO GRIP THINGS? Then you're in luck! Special end-effectors called grippers use magnets, vacuums, or movable fingers like pincers or claws to grip things so the robot can pick things up or move them around. Some end-effectors are more like tools. Roboticists have a huge toolbox to choose from when building their bots.

STEP FOUR: MAKE IT SEE!

When we leave a robot alone to do a job, we need to make sure it knows where it is.

IMAGINE THIS:

Imagine if your eyes and ears were covered and you couldn't reach out to feel your way around. You would probably bump into a lot of things. You'd probably fall over and make a huge mess, and nobody wants that!

Robots are the same! A robot shouldn't be clumsy, but it would be without sensors.

HOW DO ROBOTS SENSE THINGS?

If you need a robot to move around a lot, then it needs sensors to know where it's going. Robot sensors are a bit like our senses.You know, sight, smell, touch, sound, and taste?

Robots can't see like we can. They don't have eyes or ears, and they can't feel things in the same way that humans do. Scientists have figured out ways to make robots know what's around them and where they're going without human eyes, ears, or touch.

LIGHT SENSORS AND CAMERAS

These are a bit like our eyes. Eyes let us see what's around us and robots use light sensors to tell the difference between light and dark and to detect any obstacles that might be in their way.

SOUND SENSORS

These are like our ears. Sound sensors are a bit like microphones and robots can use them to "hear" sounds.

These kinds of robots are always listening out for you, ready to follow your instructions – just like a good little dog.

TRY THIS:

When you touch this book, does it feel rough or smooth? Hard or soft? You use your skin to feel things. The tiny little hairs on your skin help you to feel things, too.

You won't be surprised to hear that robots don't have skin. Instead, they have contact sensors. These help to stop robots from bumping, bashing, and crashing into things.

They can also tell robots how much pressure they're applying. If they need to touch something very lightly, these contact sensors help them to know how much pressure is too much pressure!

STEP FIVE: GIVE IT POWER!

Do you ever feel so hungry your stomach could burst? Your stomach might rumble and grumble and gurgle and make lots of loud, embarrassing noises. You might feel weak or tired or a bit dizzy. Maybe you even get a bit grumpy. Or very grumpy.

When we feel hungry, that's our body telling us we need to eat. We eat to give our bodies important fuel to give us energy and keep us going, so we can do all the things we want to do. Eating food is how we get our power.

Robots don't have stomachs, and they don't need to eat, but they do need a kind of power. Nothing can work without power!

HOW ARE ROBOTS POWERED?

Most robots are powered by electricity. These robots either have batteries or can be plugged into a power outlet in the wall. Electricity is pretty powerful stuff! It's made in power stations by burning coal, oil, or gas. Sometimes, we use energy from the Sun, the wind, or flowing water to make electricity.

Electricity can make robots light up, make a sound, move around, and do all the other things we need them to do!

When a robot needs more power, a low power light might come on, it might start beeping, or it might stop working altogether – just like how you might fall asleep when you're very, very tired.

Humans aren't powered by electricity like robots are. But our bodies do use tiny electrical signals to help us function. Big electricity though – like the kind in power lines – is a whole different story!

DISCLAIMER:

It can be VERY DANGEROUS, so watch out! Have you ever seen lightning? You know, that REALLY BRIGHT flash in the sky during a storm? Well, that's actually electricity, just the natural kind! It really packs a punch, so, while it's fun to do the robot dance, playing with electricity is no fun at all.

STEP SIX: FIX THE INSIDES!

- [x] So, by now, your robot has a body – CHECK!
- [x] It has legs or wheels or wings, or some kind of other parts that it can use to move – CHECK!
- [x] It has manipulators and end effectors – CHECK!
- [x] It has sensors to know where it's going – CHECK!
- [ ] All that's missing is... Wait a second...

The outside of this robot looks good to go, but there's nothing inside. Its head is full of air!

How do we know what to do or where to go, or how to talk, walk, work, or play? Have a think using your noodle, your noggin, your old gray matter... Any ideas? That's right – we use our brains! You clever brainbox, you!

Robots don't have fleshy, meaty brains like we do. Instead, programmers (or computer scientists) write out instructions for robots to follow. These are called computer programs and they act a bit like an electronic, robotic brain. Most robots have a computer processor inside them. This controls all the other parts of the robot (see, I said it was like your brain!).

Computers don't understand words that we use, so computer programs are written in computer languages. The program is then sent to the computer processor, and it uses the program to tell all the bits of the robot what to do.

Just like us, the computer processor can remember things! It stores the computer program in its memory, so the robot is ready to follow the program whenever we need it to.

WHAT IS ARTIFICIAL INTELLIGENCE?

Artificial intelligence (AI) is what we call it when machines are able to learn things using computer programs and use this to solve problems. Some robots use AI to work on their own. These robots might not be as creative, imaginative, or as kind as you, but they're definitely super-smart!

STEP SEVEN: TELL IT WHAT TO DO!

So, computer scientists are very clever and write the computer programs that robots follow. But wait! If computers can't speak human languages, and we don't know how to speak computer languages, how can we control robots?

Robots are for everyone, and it's not just computer scientists who can give them instructions and tell them what to do. When we use a robot, it's not like two people trying to talk to each other who don't speak the same language. Human-robot interface is all about how humans and robots interact with each other. The roboticists who specialize in this have a very important job.

WHAT IS AN INPUT?

Roboticists design robots with inputs. Inputs are the parts of a robot that take in information about the world around them and send this info to the computer processor inside. Remember the different types of sensors some robots have? Well, those are all examples of inputs! Buttons and remote controls are other types of inputs.

WHAT IS AN OUTPUT?

Outputs are the bits of a robot that are told what to do by the computer processor. These might be lights, sounds, or motors to make the robot move. See that flashing light? That's an output! The button to turn it on and off is the input!

Uh, that's enough now Dave. Thanks.

We press the button to turn the light on and off, and the robot knows what to do because of the computer program that's written in a language it understands.

Robots can be controlled using buttons and remote controls that are very nearby. Sometimes, they can be controlled from very far away – even from another country! This is called teleoperation.

Some robots don't need much control from humans at all.

These robots are autonomous (meaning they can complete tasks without human intervention or control) and they use their sensors to see what's around them. They use preprogrammed instructions and can sometimes use AI to adapt to new situations.

Robots aren't just a load of random bits and bobs put together – roboticists are much cleverer than that! A robot needs the right kinds of bits and bobs so that it can do its job.

Animals are like this, too! Different animals are specialized to live in different habitats, eat different things, or move in different ways.

Animals are experts in specialization. in fact, they're so good at this, some roboticists are looking at animals for inspiration when building their robots, especially when they're looking at how to solve problems of the future! This is called...

BIOMIMETIC, BIOMIMICRY, OR BIONIC ROBOTICS.

Have you ever seen an octopus? Well, they're pretty cool. Did you know octopuses don't have bones in their bodies? Some octopuses are HUGE, and even the biggest octopus in the ocean has no bones in its body. Not a single one! These slippery, slimy, squishy sea monsters are able to fit into very small spots, all thanks to their squishy bodies!

INVENTION: OCTOBOTS

In 2016, scientists at Harvard University in the USA created something INCREDIBLE – the first EVER autonomous, completely soft robot. Robots don't usually have bones, but they do have lots of hard bits like batteries, wires, and bits made of metal. Well, just like an octopus, this robot is completely soft and squishy. And, it has no electronics! **Wait, are we sure this isn't actually an octopus?** This robot is so similar to a real octopus that it's been nicknamed Octobot. Octobot was made using a 3D printer. A chemical reaction inside Octobot changes its tiny bit of liquid fuel into a HUGE amount of gas (no, not that kind of gas!). This gas rushes into Octobot's arms and blows them up like a big balloon – no electricity necessary!

INVENTION: ROBOBEE

Harvard University is also home to another bio-inspired bot much smaller than Octobot. This tiny robot is called RoboBee and it looks like... well... a bee! It has flapping wings that help it move in the air and in water. It's inspired by flying bugs and sea plankton, and is changing the game in microrobotics!

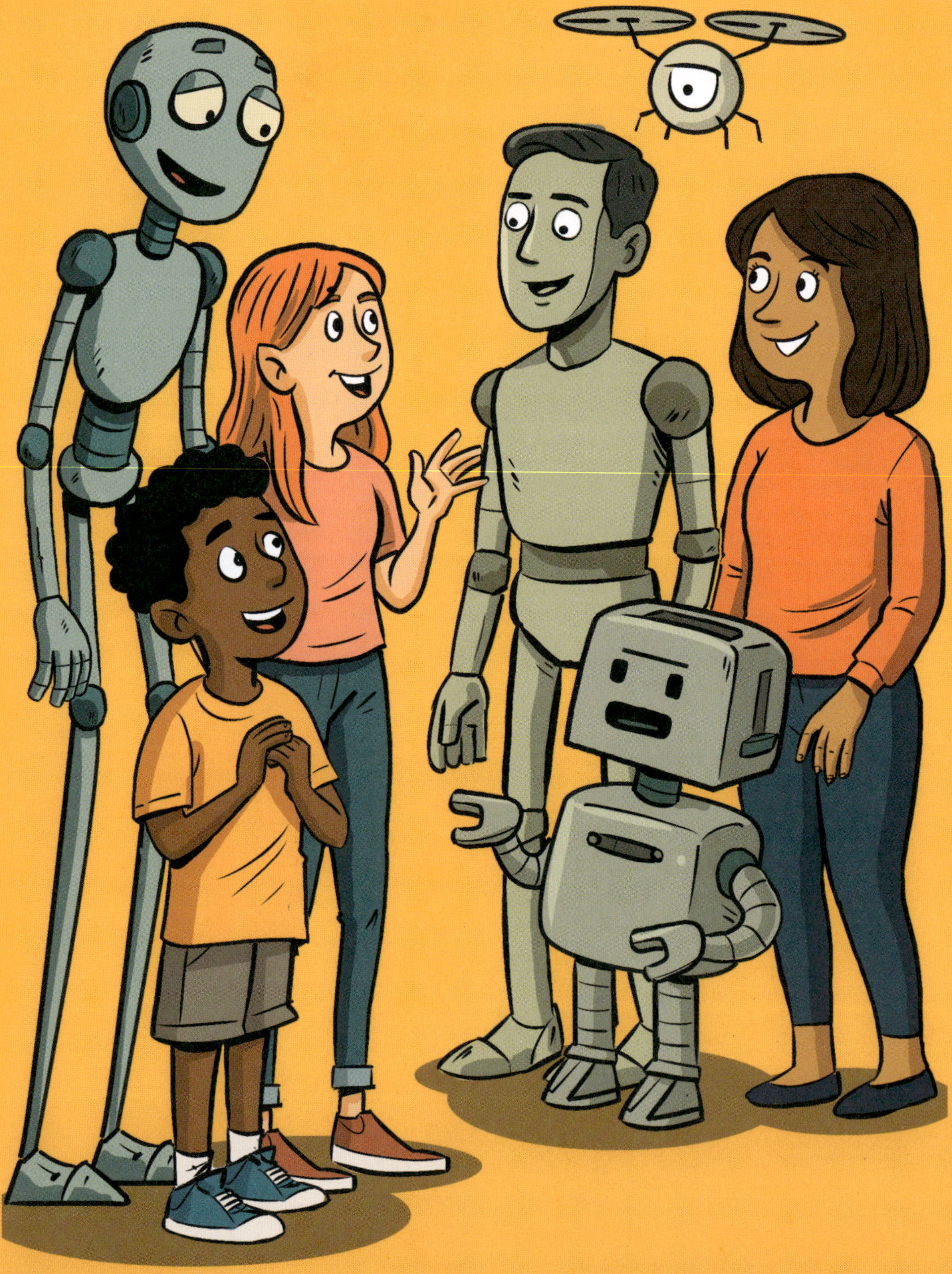

Chapter 3

WELCOME TO THE FAMILY!

Not all robots are blasting off into outer space or being used by super-intelligent scientists for top-secret, life-saving missions; lots of robots are used by normal, everyday people like you and me, for very normal, everyday jobs.

Does that mean the days of doing boring chores could be over?! That's right – robots are here to save the day, just not the world this time.

HOMEBOTS

Homebots are robots that live and work in, you guessed it, our homes. These robots are so normal that you might not even guess they're robots by looking at them.

Some of these homebots might not be very exciting to look at, but the science behind them is really changing the game!

Scientists have been working together to build homebots with some pretty out-of-this-world technology. They won't be taking us into the cosmos, but they can clean our homes, cook our dinner, and even do our laundry.

Sound boring? Well, if homebots are taking on the boring jobs around our homes, that means we have more time for more exciting things.

IMAGINE THIS:

If a robot could do your homework, what could you do instead? Maybe you'd spend more time playing videogames with your friends, or perhaps you'd become a world-famous explorer, traveling the globe in search of rare and exotic animals.

Or maybe you have a top-secret plan for taking over the world, and all you need is a bit of time to put these plans into action...

Well, put those dreams away – world domination will just have to wait! Robots are incredible, but we don't have homework robots yet. And anyway, if there's one thing you should always be doing without a robot's help, it's your homework!

If you're thinking these robots don't look very futuristic or particularly high tech, well, that's kind of the point! These robots are designed especially to look friendly and not too out-of-place in our homes.

Roboticists think a lot about how a robot works, but they also need to think about how a robot looks.

Would you trust a robot to help you if it looked too scary? Just think, it might look a bit odd if there was some big, fancy robot in your house. With no face and just claws and levers and wheels, it would probably be more at home on a spaceship or in a factory than at your dinner table!

These robots are supposed to look friendly and approachable, especially humanoid homebots. When robots are working alongside us and living in our homes, it's really important that we trust them and that we feel safe with them. This is exactly why androids are designed to look like us.

PEPPER

Meet Pepper. Standing at only 1.2 meters (4 feet) high and with big, puppy-dog eyes and the sweetest little smile, Pepper is simply ADORABLE. Pepper is a companion robot, and this means it's basically there to be our friend. Just like a good friend, Pepper knows how you're feeling, whether that's happy, sad, angry, or surprised!

Rather than using eyes and ears, Pepper uses special cameras and sensors to read your face and the tone of your voice. If it senses that you're sad, Pepper might try to make you feel better with a silly joke.

Pepper doesn't spend all its time joking around, though – it's built to work in offices, shops, hotels, schools, and anywhere else it can connect with people like you and me.

Many of the robots that work in our homes are smart, but not "smart" as in clever. Well, they are very clever, but that's not the kind of smart we're talking about here. When we talk about smart technology, we're talking about normal, everyday devices that have been powered up to become...

SUPER DEVICES!

SMART DEVICES

You might have heard of smartphones, but what about smart watches, smart refrigerators, and even smart vacuum cleaners?

You're probably wondering how a fridge or a vacuum cleaner can be "smart". What exactly would a powered-up super vacuum cleaner be like? Well, just like robots, smart devices are designed to make our lives easier and more automated. They might do this by using the internet, machine learning, or artificial intelligence.

SMARTPHONES

Smartphones are a very common type of smart technology. While you can only really use a cellphone to call your friends or send a text message, smartphones can do so much more!

All smartphones are cellphones, but not all cellphones are smartphones. Normal cellphones are pretty basic, but smartphones are on another level!

Want to surf the web? Download some apps? Make a videocall? Control your robot vacuum cleaner?! You're in luck – smartphones can do all of these things, and more!

But wait – smartphones aren't robots, are they?
No, they're not, but some smart devices are robots!

These smart devices and robots work great on their own, but they're even better when they're connected. When lots of devices are connected and work together to run your super smart home, it's called the internet of things.

IMAGINE THIS:

Imagine a home where your smart doorbell sends a message to your smartphone to tell you your friend is at the door, while you're watching a movie recommended by your smart TV, and your smart vacuum cleaner is clearing up the mess from your popcorn. That's pretty smart!

Smart homes are the homes of the future, and nifty little robots like Pepper (and some less-cute robots too) play a very important part.

Some very clever roboticists have been working very hard to fully automate our lives, so now there is pretty much a homebot for every job you can think of! What helpful little bots.

Not all smart devices are robots, but the best homebots are the ones that use smart technology to connect to other robots and smart devices in our homes.

Think of it like a big surprise party. All the robots and smart devices in your home are constantly talking to each other and sharing information about you, all without you even noticing!

Some robots are needier than others and don't like to be left alone for too long. Autonomous robot vacuum cleaners are not needy at all – they're great at being left alone!

AUTONOMOUS ROBOT CLEANERS

They are small, round, and flat, with little wheels for getting around – perfect for fitting under sofas and not getting stuck.

They zip around to create a map of your home, keeping track of any furniture and obstacles. They store this map in their computer brain and use it to find their way around. They can set themselves off on their way, or they can be controlled from a smartphone using smart technology.

Don't panic if things get moved around. Robot vacuums use infrared and contact sensors so there'll be no robo-casualties here!

IMPORTANT WORDS TO KNOW:

Infrared sensors use light. Infrared light is reflected from objects, and the objects then send a signal back to the robot.

Contact sensors are on a robot's bumpers. If the sensor goes off, the robot will know to stay away.

When they run out of charge, they use infrared signals to find their charging base so they can take themselves off to bed to charge themselves up, ready for another cleaning session. How independent! Sure, independent, autonomous robots are great for when there's a chore you don't want to do yourself, but what about if you're feeling lonely and you want a robot to keep you company?

Remember Pepper? Well, there are lots of other companion robots just waiting to meet you and become your new best friend.

Robots don't just exist to work on their own. They may not get lonely like humans do, but lots of robots actually work better alongside people.

Some robots have been created to teach kids all about robots and coding. These robots look a bit like robot vacuum cleaners, but don't worry – they won't be sucking anything up. These bots are here to play!

It's really important that the next generation of super-scientists know how to code, and these little robots are here to teach us how to do just that!

BUT, WHAT IS CODING?

Coding, or computer programming, is how we create instructions and tell a computer, or robot, what to do. This can be very complicated, and it can sometimes take whole teams of very clever scientists to write the code for one robot.

BEE-BOTS

These funny little floor bots have round bodies and tiny wheels. They were created to help children learn how to code. They have lots of buttons all over their bodies that we can use to tell them where to do and what to do.

If you want the robot to go forward, press the forward button! And if you want it to go left, press the left button! And for it to go right? That's right! I mean, correct!

These robots are very obedient and will do whatever you program them to do, in the order you press the buttons!

Just like the buttons on the floor bot, when we create code for a computer or robot to follow, it always follows the instructions in order from the top,
to the next line,
and the next line,
and the next,
all the way
down
to the bottom.

When you know how to write code to control robots, the possibilities are endless! You could make robots do whatever you want, whenever you want!

CODING CREATIONS

Hold onto your bots, because some clever roboticists have been using their coding know-how to create robots that know how to play some very complicated games.

CHESS-TASTIC ROBOTS

Do you know how to play chess? What about Go? Well, it doesn't matter if you don't know how to play, because this robots can teach you!

AI algorithms are sets of instructions or rules, and this little robot uses these to decide what moves to make, and uses its robotic arm and three-finger claw to pick up chess pieces and move them across the board.

It may not look like your typical teacher or opponent, but one robot from China is SO GOOD at playing chess that it's beaten chess Grand Masters and has now partnered up with the European Chess Union to help teach chess all over Europe. The days of human vs. human chess games could soon be in the past!

So, robots are excellent at socializing and great at playing games. Obviously, not all social robots look like us – but did you know some actually look like our pets?!

PET OR ROBOT?

Ever fancied a sweet little Fluffy or Fido, but been too worried about the fur getting EVERYWHERE? Or maybe you're allergic, and any cuddles would leave you all...

Well, here is the answer to all of your problems! A sweet little friend you can walk, cuddle, and play with, and don't need to worry about forgetting to feed or pick up after?

Perfect! These four-legged robots can walk, bark, meow, and purr using interactive sensors, and some of them even have sweet little faces and soft, strokable fur.

Some scientists have found that these robotic pets can make people feel calmer, happier, and less anxious. Good boy!

But wait, there's more! Robots aren't just great company – we can also use them to help us get around.

DRIVERLESS DRIVING

Fancy a ride? That's right – robot cars are taking over our streets. These robots look just like ordinary cars, except there's no driver!

Autonomous robotic cars use radar (instruments that detect objects using radio waves), cameras, and LiDAR sensors that can detect lane markings, curbs, pedestrians, cyclists, or other cars, just like your eyes can! These sensors can send signals to the car's insides and tell it to brake, steer, or accelerate.

LiDAR sensors fire light to different objects and the objects then reflect the light back. It works out how long it took for the light to get reflected back and uses this to calculate the distance between the sensors and the object.

BUT, WHAT IS LIDAR?

LiDAR stands for Light Detection And Ranging and is used in robots all over the world. It was invented by a team of scientists in 1962 and since then it's been used in airplanes, spacecraft, self-driving cars, and robot vacuum cleaners!

FUN FACT: APOLLO 15

In 1971, Apollo 15 became the fourth crewed mission to land on our closest space neighbor, the Moon. The scientists behind Apollo 15 used LiDAR to measure the distance between the Apollo 15 spacecraft and the surface of the Moon.

From space technology to the robots in your living room, so many of the robots of today wouldn't work without LiDAR.

Autonomous robots don't just need to know where obstacles are, though – they need to know what and where they're trying to get to. If you're out and about exploring a new place, you might use a map to find your way around. Sometimes robots use maps, too!

DELIVERY ROBOTS

Autonomous delivery robots are like self-driving cars but smaller. Instead of driving people around, they drive themselves along sidewalks and deliver food, drinwk, and parcels across towns and cities and straight to your front door.

Scientists draw lots of maps for these robots using simple lines and paths. They don't hold them in their hands like you would, though. The maps are stored in their computer memory and, because they're robots and a robot's memory is a lot better than yours, they never forget where to go.

These little delivery bots rarely get lost. They use the maps drawn by scientists, their own photos and videos they take while out and about, and live feedback from their sensors to create 3D maps of where they are.

DELIVERY DRONES

Hey, look up. See that? Watch your head! That's a delivery drone on its way to deliver your mail. Well, maybe not your mail, but definitely someone's mail! Delivery drones are autonomous aerial vehicles (AAVs), and they're great for getting things to people who live in hard-to-reach places.

One delivery drone nicknamed Parcelcopter is changing the lives of people who live on Ukerewe Island on Lake Victoria in Tanzania, Africa. It can take 6 hours to get medicine to Ukerewe Island by boat, but Parcelcopter is slashing this time! Safety pilots upload mission pathways to Parcelcopter, and it uses this map to deliver life-saving medicine in under an hour.

ANOTHER DAY, ANOTHER ROBOT SAVING THE WORLD!

From companion bots to smart technology, robot pets, self-driving cars, and AAVs, robots are really making themselves at home in our homes. They can keep us company, teach us chess, drive us around, and deliver our mail and medicine. Some homebots already look like they're straight out of a sci-fi film, so what could the future of homebots possibly look like?!

Homebots like Pepper are great at being our friend, but there's only so much they can do. We can get different robots to cook us dinner, make our beds, do our laundry, and clean our floors, but can you imagine if there was one robot to do all of these jobs?

ENTER THE SMART HOME ROBOT BUTLER!

Imagine a robot that could wake you up in the morning, cook you breakfast, drop you off at school, walk your robotic dog, clean your home, and be there at the end of the day to play with you and tuck you in to bed. Sound like a dream? Well, it might be real one day!

Smart home butlers are already popping up in homes around the world, but these voice-activated personal assistants aren't robots. They may be able to control your lights, check your security cameras, and tap into other parts of your smart home, but they can't move around like a robot butler would be able to do.

Take a look at your hands. They can grip, lift, push, pull, carry, pick, and twist. Robot butlers wouldn't specialize in one job – they'd be able to do them all! They would need end-effectors that would allow them to do all of these different jobs, just like human hands!

32 DAYS
ACCIDENT
FREE.

Chapter 4
WORKING HARD LIKE A HUMAN

Human beings are very hardworking. There are lots of jobs we have to do to keep our world up and running, and to make sure our fellow humans are happy and healthy.

THINK ABOUT THIS...

Have you ever thought about where your food comes from? No, I don't mean your fridge. Think back further... before it gets to your home, and even before it gets to the store, where does food really come from?

All the food we eat, every single bit, needs to be grown and made somewhere, and with over eight billion people on our planet to feed, it's not an easy job!

And what about all the things we use every day? Things like cars, books, pens, clothes, and toys... every single one of these things needs to be made by someone! Most of these things are made in factories and shipped around the world before they land in your waiting hands.

Growing all of this food and making all of these things is a tough job for humans. Humans get tired and need lots of breaks and, compared to robots, they're not very strong at all.

Every human gets tired after too much work, and every human needs breaks to use the bathroom, have a snack, or even just be a little bit silly for a while.

If only there were something that could help us!

You read my mind, small human factory worker! There is something that can help, and that something is robots!

INDUSTRIAL OR MANUFACTURING ROBOTS

Industrial and manufacturing robots are ones we use for making things in factories. These robots are automated, programmable, and movable. They're usually designed to do boring, repetetive, or dangerous jobs.

AGRICULTURAL ROBOTS

Forget the traditional ways of farming, agricultural robots are the hot, new names on the farm! These robots might harvest crops, spray pesticides, milk cows, or zap weeds.

Back in the day, before the wonders of our robot helpers, factories looked very different. Making things was a very **S L O W** process. Factories were full of big, heavy machinery, and people stood on production lines tapping, hammering, and welding.

The work was **very** slow, **very** boring, and **very** repetitive.

Ok, we get it!

Not only was it slow and repetitive, it was actually really dangerous! When people get tired, they can make mistakes. Some mistakes don't matter too much, like putting your clothes on the wrong way round. This might be embarrassing, and you might not be able to show your face for a while after showing up to school with your pants on back to front, but at least nothing too bad will happen.

IMAGINE THIS...

You're working in a factory and you've been doing the same, boring task for hours and hours already. It's nice and warm, and you're feeling nice and comfortable. Your eyes feel heavy and you start to feel sleepy, and before you know it... **DISASTER**.

Not to be dramatic, but making mistakes in a factory really could be life or death!

NOW, YOU KNOW WHO DOESN'T GET TIRED? THAT'S RIGHT – **ROBOTS.**

Unimate was the first robot to ever be used in a factory, way back in the 1960s. These robots could do jobs that were too difficult, dangerous, or boring for human workers.

Now our factories are FULL of robots. Robots that don't get tired, don't need breaks, and work quicker (and sometimes more safely) than human workers!

More robots in our factories means more things can be made. Hooray! And it could make the factories safer for the humans working there, too. Double hooray!

When scientists design industrial robots, they have to make sure they have all the right parts in all the right places. Humans have handy hands and fiddly fingers that are great at picking things up and moving things around.

Our fingers and hands are so good at doing some jobs that scientists have designed robots that have dainty and delicate digits just like us (try saying that three times fast!).

ROBOTIC FINGERS?

When robots have fingers, we don't actually call them fingers. Well, you can, and people will know what you're talking about, but if you want to pretend you're a robotics expert, call them...

END OF ARM TOOLING, OR EOAT

for short. End of arm tooling is anything attached to the end of a robot's arm to help it do a useful job.

Remember end-effectors? Well, these are types of EOAT and they're very important in all robots, including manufacturing robots.

Grippers, tools, and sensors are all end-effectors, and they can be adapted to the job you need a robot to do. Need a robot that can spray paint a car? Great! There's an end-effector for that. What about a robot that can weld one bit of a car onto another bit? You guessed it – bring me that end-effector!

What about a robot that can pick your nose, pop a balloon, and stroke your pet hamster, all in that order?

Don't be disgusting! But maybe, yes. But now we're just getting silly, and EOAT is serious business.

BAXTER

Baxter is a robot that is here to do its job and do it well. It was the first ever dual-arm robot designed to work alongside people. Put your end-effectors in the air for Baxter!

Baxter might not have hands, but it does have a vacuum cup and a gripper with things that work like fingers. It even has a computer screen head that shows its human factory coworkers what it's up to by displaying different cartoony expressions.

EOAT IS REALLY IMPORTANT.

For robots working in factories, different end-effectors are needed for different jobs:

- For picking and placing, **GRIPPERS** can grip, grasp, and move things from one place to another. If you see a robot on an assembly line, it will probably have grippers! These grippers might be mechanical, vacuum, or magnetic.
- Need a robot to do a more specific job? Make way for the **PROCESS TOOLS.** Welding guns, paint spray guns, cutting tools, and grinding tools are all types of process tools.
- **ROBOTIC FORCE COMPLIANCE END-EFFECTORS** can help robots grip and move things very, very carefully.
- **SENSORS** like proximity sensors, force sensors, cameras, and light sensors tell a robot where it is and what's around it.

SO THAT EXPLAINS THE OUTSIDE OF A WORKER ROBOT, BUT WHAT ABOUT THE INSIDE?

Jobs in a factory can sometimes involve doing the same thing again and again and again, and the robots that do these jobs need to be very accurate and very precise. There's no room for mistakes here!

Lots of industrial robots are programmed with pick-and-place programs.

WHAT IS A PICK-AND-PLACE PROGRAM?

This is when a robot picks up an object and places it in a new location. These robots might pick and place hundreds or even thousands of times every single hour!

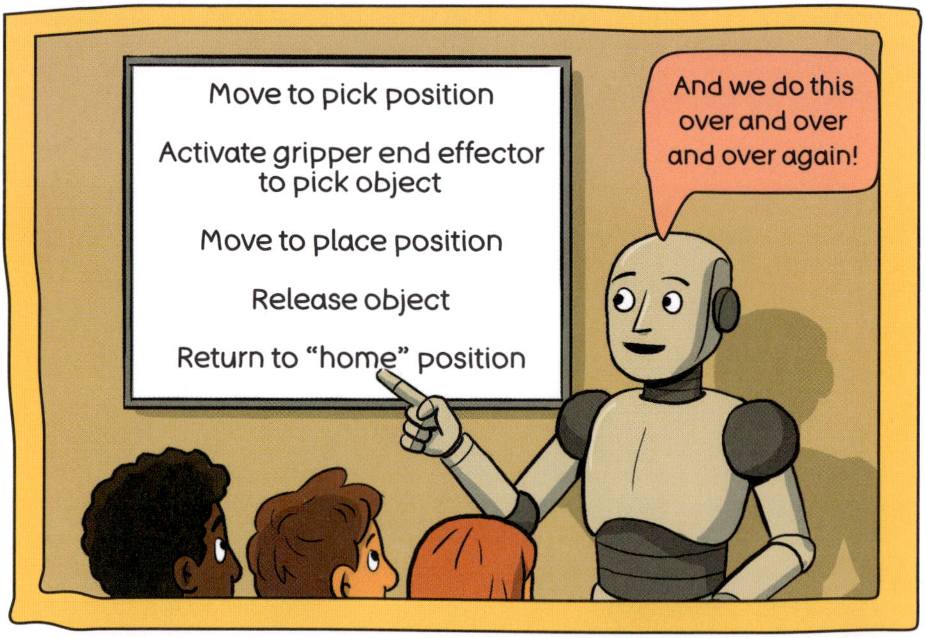

This pick-and-place program is simple enough for a robot to remember and and repeat again and again, very quickly. It's a good thing robots don't get bored!

Sometimes, things don't just need to be moved about on an assembly line. Sometimes they need to be moved from one side of a factory to another.

This might not seem like a big deal if it's just something small. But what if it's a whole car, or a great, big box that's even bigger than you?

PROBLEM: TACKLING BIG JOBS

In a factory or warehouse, things need to always be moving smoothly so that nothing ever stops. Logistics is all about moving things around in the right way and at the right time to make sure things are always where they need to be.

WHY IS IT A PROBLEM?

But humans need to stop sometimes – they need bathroom breaks, they get tired, and they might sometimes make mistakes. And when the things that need to be moved around are big and heavy, it could take humans a very long time to shove and heave these things around.

WHAT ARE WE DOING ABOUT IT?

With robots, logistics becomes a lot easier.

BRING IN THE REINFORCEMENTS.

In a warehouse full of boxes and packages, robots can zip around and use their computer brains to find exactly where something is, before picking it up and taking it to the right place. All before you've even said:

ANOTHER WIN FOR ROBOTS EVERYWHERE!

Robots are great at gripping, grasping, lifting, and moving. They don't need breaks to eat or sleep, and they rarely need to stop at all. They're a lot stronger than humans, and once programmed with a task, they can work completely on their own.

Human workers might get distracted, but not robots!

Buildings were designed for humans – they have narrow spaces and tight corners that it would be a squeeeeze to get big, bulky robots into.

Humans are great at squeezing round corners and shuffling around tight spots, but sometimes a job would get done a lot faster if a robot could take a human's place. If only there were a small, human-shaped super-strong robot helper that could help us out...

DIGIT

Thanks to some very clever scientists, there are lots of these robots ready to lend a helping end-effector (see what I did there?). Digit might not look much like a human, but with a head, a torso, two arms, and two legs, it's close enough!

Digit can lift, move, stack, unstack, and sort. It can lift big, heavy loads and zip around busy buildings, round corners, and into tight spaces without bumping into things, tripping over, or getting tired. Thanks to the scientists that built it, Digit is doing such a good job that Time Magazine named it one of the best inventions of 2024! Way to go, Digit!

So, it looks like our factories and warehouses might soon be full of robots. This might also be the case for our farms one day too!

What would you usually expect to see on a farm? Maybe some cows, some chickens, a sheep or two, a field of crops, maybe some tractors, a robot...

A FARM ROBOT?

Well, actually, yes! Robots are being used to plow fields, plant seeds, harvest crops, and look after livestock, and all of this is making farming a lot faster, easier, and more efficient!

Human beings are hungry creatures. In fact, human beings never stop being hungry! Growing all the food we need takes a lot of work, so thank goodness roboticists have been busy designing clever agricultural robots to help farmers bring food from the fields to our forks!

There are so many different types of robots working on farms all around the world, each with their own special jobs.

Some of these robots work on planting, watering, weeding, and harvesting, but other robots look after the animals on the farm.

LET'S MEET SOME OF THESE AMAZING AGRICULTURAL AUTOMATONS!

MILKING ROBOTS

"I'm a milking robot! I can't mooooove, so when a cow wants to be milked, it mooooooches inside me — yes, inside! I check its tag to know which cow it is, and then I clean its udder, milk it very carefully, and then it's free to go on its way. The cows are free to come and go as they please — this means moooore milk, and happy cows!"

FEEDING ROBOTS

"Don't worry, I'm not asking for food — I do the feeding around here! I move around the barn and give the right amount of food to every animal. I make sure every animal in my barn gets the nutrition they need! Some of my feeding friends can even measure how much each animal eats and track their health. Healthy animals = happy animals = happy farmers!"

AUTONOMOUS TRACTORS

"I'm a tractor! Think you've met me before? Well, think again! I can take myself out without needing a farmer to drive me. You could say I'm autonomous, and you'd be correct! I have smart sensors and cameras that help me see where I am when I'm plowing, tilling, planting, and fertilizing."

HARVESTING ROBOTS

"Need some crops harvested? I'm your guy, with my 24 robotic arms! My built-in cameras spy out only the best strawberries, my robotic arms carefully grip and cut the stems, and LiDAR sensors make sure I'm always staying out of harm's way. I'm on a mission to help farmers everywhere harvest crops more quickly and more safely, all without damaging a single fruit. After all, 24 robotic grippers are better than one!"

WEEDING ROBOTS

"Got weeds? Not after I've been at them! There are lots of different types of weeding robots. Some use cameras and sensors to spot weeds before targeting them with just the right amount of herbicide. Now that's some smart spraying! Other weeding robots, like me, move around and churn weeds up using our scrubbing wheels. Watch out, weeds – you're no match for us!"

With the help of these fancy bots, farmers grow all the food we need to eat, but none of this would be possible without the humble honeybee.

Pollination is when pollen is spread between different flowers, and we wouldn't be able to grow food without it! Birds, bees, bats, and bugs are all pollinators, but bees are by far the most important!

BUT I COME BEARING TERRIBLE NEWS. HONEYBEES ARE IN...

GRAVE DANGER.

Honeybee colonies around the world are dying. How?! Why?! And what can we do to stop this?! Well, not even scientists are certain they have all the answers to these questions!

Scientists think that something called colony collapse disorder might affect how honeybees are able to find their way around.

COLONY COLLAPSE DISORDER?

These poor little bees leave their cozy hives to find nectar and pollen, never to return. They are lost... **FOREVER**. Farmers need honeybees to pollinate their crops, so if it's bye-bye honeybees, it's also bye-bye **ALL FOOD FOR HUMANITY**.

Surely this is a problem too big even for robots to fix? Think again! That's right – robots are back again to save us and our planet, and these little bug-bots are the bee's knees!

MICROROBOTICS

Scientists at Harvard University and MIT have created autonomous flying microrobots inspired by bees. These bug-sized bee-bots weigh less than a paperclip and could hold the key to future pollination.

With honeybees dropping like flies, scientists hope that one day these mini machines, immune to colony collapse disorder, could swarm out of mechanical hives and perform precise pollination without any hiccups.

Microrobotics is a pretty new science, so these baby bots aren't quite ready to fly solo yet, but keep an eye out for them because maybe one day they'll be filling the skies!

Chapter 5

DANGER! ROBOTS AT WORK

DISASTER! DANGER!

PICTURE THE SCENE.

All around you it's dark and dusty. Buildings have collapsed. The ground won't stop shaking. There's fire everywhere and the flames are getting closer and closer. It's so hot you can feel the sweat on your brow. You're trapped under rubble. You shout for help but nobody can hear you.

SILENCE.

You think all is lost until you feel a hand grabbing you and pulling you up. But this hand doesn't feel human. It's hard and cold and is holding you with a kind of superhuman strength.

It pulls you up and up, into the fresh, clean air and the blinding light. You turn your head to see your rescuer.

SURPRISE, SURPRISE – IT'S A ROBOT!

Scientists aren't just building robots to make our lives easier – they're actually designing robots that can save our lives!

When disasters happen, (things like earthquakes, tsunamis, hurricanes, and nuclear disasters), it can sometimes be difficult to get help to people who need it. It might be very difficult to reach the people in need (if they can even be found at all!) or it might actually be too dangerous to send people into the disaster zone.

But if robots are helping us in other industries,

WHY CAN'T THEY HELP US HERE, TOO?

ROBIN MURPHY

Robin Murphy is an expert in something called DISASTER ROBOTICS. In fact, she actually founded the whole field of disaster robotics!

Her research is focused on how humans and robots can work together to help in rescue, relief, and recovery, and she has studied or responded to around 50 emergencies around the world, looking at how robots can be used to save lives.

She co-founded **CRASAR**, the **C**enter for **R**obot-**A**ssisted **S**earch and **R**escue, and her work in disaster robotics is really changing the world! By working with other scientists, roboticists, and disaster experts, she is proving that we can use robots in revolutionary ways.

HUMANS DEAL WITH SOME PRETTY DEADLY DISASTERS. Whether it's an avalance, an earthquake, a tornado, or a volcanic eruption, disasters are happening all the time, all around the world.

Some disasters are natural, but some disasters, like oil spills and nuclear explosions, are caused by humans.

Whether a disaster is natural or not, if humans want to come out safely the other side, they'll need to clear up the big, old mess that's left behind. Believe it or not, disaster response is not an easy job.

It's actually very, very dangerous. Police and fire departments and search and rescue teams are usually the first feet on the ground when a disaster happens, and sometimes these early rescue teams are not even sure exactly what they're walking into.

What is the danger? How many people are in danger, and where are they? And where on earth is the danger?! Sometimes there's not even enough time to find out before disaster response teams are sent in for their search and rescue missions.

DISASTER ROBOTICS

Disasters can be dangerous and scary, but some super scientists have built some super robots that are risking motherboard and manipulator to get us out alive.

DRONES

Drones are unmanned aerial vehicles (UAVs) and this means they can fly without an on-board pilot, which is great news for disaster robotics! They can be fitted with night and day cameras, sensors, thermal imaging technology, and even communication systems.

They can be controlled remotely or fly autonomously and be used to scout out danger, assess the disaster damage, and spot people who need to be rescued, all without setting foot in the disaster zone.

LAND ROBOTS

Land robots can use tracks, wheels, and even legs to clamber over difficult ground to get to hard-to-reach places. Some surface-rescue robots are even able to float and swim. It looks like no disaster is too big or too dangerous for these brave little bots, but maybe we shouldn't put that to the test!

Sometimes it rains, and sometimes it pours. Sometimes it rains so much that rivers might burst their banks and suddenly there's water where there really shouldn't be water. And not just clean water, either. When towns and cities flood, the water can be really dirty and really dangerous. Leave your bathing suit at home – you definitely don't want to be paddling in this!

This water might end up in homes, schools, and shops. It might wash away cars, trees, and even people. A tiny drop of water might not seem like much, but when lots of these tiny droplets team up, water becomes super powerful. When people get caught up in floods, it could end up in, you guessed it, disaster!

WATER RESCUE ROBOTS

Water rescue robots are covering above and below water. They can use sonar technology to send pulses of sound below the water to find obstacles they need to avoid and people they need to rescue. Sounds neat! These bots are ready to help wherever there's water, whether that's in flooded areas or even at sea.

ROBOT: DOLPHIN-1

Dolphin-1 is an unmanned surface vehicle (USV) already saving lives in China. Despite its name, Dolphin 1, a kind of remote-controlled robotic lifebuoy, doesn't look much like waterborne mammal. It actually looks more like a surfing rocket!

ROBOT RESCUE

In 2022, when a teenager was swept out to sea by a strong undercurrent in Weihai, China, Dolphin-1 was sent out to save the day. The waves were too strong for a human to battle, but Dolphin-1 found it no problem at all. That's right – this story has a happy ending! Not only was Dolphin-1 strong enough to ride the waves, it successfully pulled the sea-swept teenager safely back to shore.

HOORAY FOR ROBOTS!

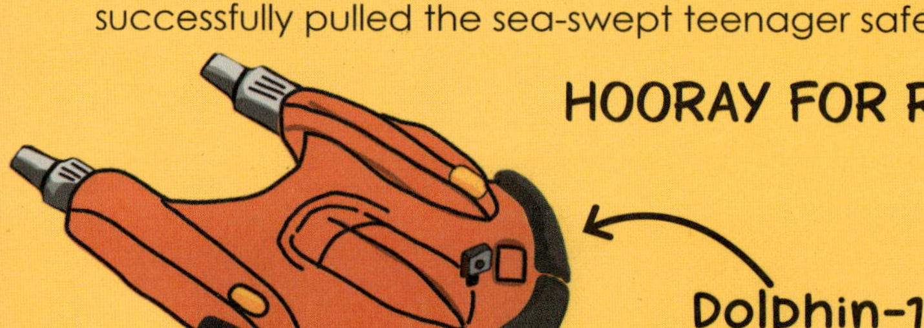

ROBOT: EMILY

EMILY, or Emergency Integrated Lifesaving Lanyard (but that's just not as snappy), is another remote-controlled water rescue bot. EMILY can really make a splash and be dropped from the air into the water. What an entrance! It's powered forward by an electric motor and is so strong it can carry up to five adults at any time – no one gets left behind!

PROBLEM: DEEP DARK WATERS

Water can be deep, dark, and scary. If someone's floating on the surface, they might not be too hard to find, but what if there's someone under the water who needs saving? Someone under the water at night?

WHY IS IT A PROBLEM?

If it's dark, or if someone could be trapped where we might not be able to see them straight away, our eyes just aren't enough! Even normal cameras might miss people sometimes.

WHAT ARE WE DOING ABOUT IT?

Well, scientists are looking into how EMILY might be able to use thermal imaging cameras in the future to help with this very problem. Everything gives off heat, and thermal imaging cameras see this heat instead of light and turn it into a picture. Warm things show up as red or yellow and cooler things are blue or purple. You might not be able to see lots of detail with a thermal imaging camera, but you can see colorful, human-shaped blobs, and that's better than seeing nothing at all!

Some rescue bots, like rescue drones, are already helping us find people our meagre little human eyes would never be able to spot. Some rescue drones are kitted out to the max with infrared and daylight cameras, thermal imaging cameras, and radar technology to make sure they're not flying into anything they shouldn't be.

Drones are helping rescue missions all over the world and giving rescue teams a bird's-eye view of the danger below. They're even being used by firefighters to see through the smoke and stream real-time footage so they know exactly where to go.

Drones might be great at showing us what's happening from above, but sometimes we need to head back down to earth and send ground robots in to give us a different perspective... search, rescue, and recovery missions are serious stuff.

Rescue robots need to be able to move around and move quickly in all different kinds of places and across different kinds of terrain.

SCIENTISTS GIVE THESE ROBOTS THE VERY BEST LEGS, TRACKS, AND WHEELS SO NO TERRAIN IS TOO TOUGH!

- Sometimes robots have tracks like you'd usually find on a tank or a bulldozer. Tracks have lots of grip and are great for moving over sand, snow, rubble, or other rough and bumpy ground.

- Robots with wheels are usually low to the ground, and their wheels can get stuck on mud and rocks, so these are usually great for moving quickly over flat ground like roads and sidewalks.

- Legs are great for climbing over rocks and rubble or jumping up and down stairs. Some robots have two legs like a human. For ground that is too rough or bumpy for our legs, scientists have built quadruped robots that have four legs, and some robots that have six!

Animals with four legs are much better at climbing than two-legged humans (mountain goats are called mountain goats for a reason!), so multi-legged robots are very important for helping out in disasters.

DEEP ROBOTICS LYNX

With its little body and four legs, DEEP Robotics Lynx might look like a robot dog, but it's actually a super high-tech rescue robot built for saving lives! It can walk, run, and climb all over places that other robots or even humans might get stuck in.

It's got cameras, thermal sensors, and LiDAR that all help it find people a lot faster than a human rescue team could.

What makes this robot really special, though, is that it doesn't just have four legs. It has four legs with wheels!

Lynx can climb over rocks, boulders, and rubble and even use its wheels to run and slide down hills at very high speeds. For this robot, four legs are better than two, and four wheeled legs are even better!

Sometimes, sending one robot on a rescue mission isn't enough. Just think, you'd never send in one person on their own to do a scary, difficult, or dangerous job. With humans, teamwork makes the dream work, and sometimes the same is true of robots!

Except, when robots work together to get a job done, we don't call it teamwork. Sometimes, when robots work together, they do it using... **SWARM TECHNOLOGY!** Exactly like a swarm of bees!

SWARM TECHNOLOGY

Swarm technology is inspired by ants, bees, termites, and flocks of birds. These little animals might not be able to achieve much on their own, but when they work together, they can do so much more!

With swarm robots, there's no big boss. Instead, it's like the bots all share one, huge brain. They can communicate and share information using wireless signals like radio or infrared. They all follow the same, simple rules and can learn from each other and then adapt to what's around them. When they work together, they can get the job done faster!

These helpful hives could be the future of search and rescue robotics, and some scientists have been working hard to create some that could one day be used to search for people after a disaster.

ZEBRO

Scientists at TU Delft in the Netherlands have created a type of six-legged swarm robot they are calling Zebro. When one Zebro finds something interesting or someone who needs help, it can send out a signal to the closest other Zebro which can then pass on the signal to another Zebro. The swarm can then create a path that can lead rescue teams to where they need to be.

Zebro isn't quite ready for search and rescue missions yet, but one day these little bots could be the next big superhero disaster squad.

Sometimes it's not just the ground that's unsafe after a disaster.

Can you imagine if even the air around you could kill you?

(Yikes)

Well, buckle up – we're heading into the world of

NUCLEAR DISASTERS.

WHAT IS NUCLEAR ENERGY?

Nuclear energy is the energy that holds together the nucleus of an atom. Not sure what an atom is? Atoms are basically the building blocks of every single thing EVER. Everything, and I mean everything, is made up of atoms, and every atom has a nucleus at its center.

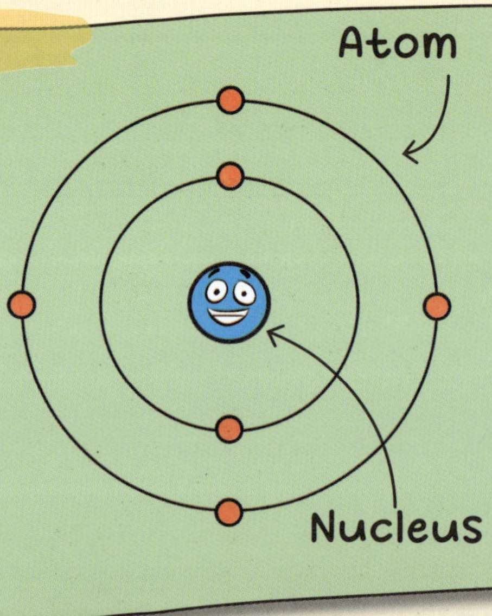

Some crazy clever scientists figured out how to break a nucleus apart, and they called this process **NUCLEAR FISSION.**

This releases loads of energy that changes into other types of energy called radiation.

We can use nuclear fission in nuclear power plants to create heat that we can then use to create electricity. Nuclear power plants produce lots of radioactive waste that can be really dangerous if we ever get too close to itv. These power plants are designed to be safe, but sometimes accidents happen.

FUKUSHIMA DISASTER

In 2011, the most powerful earthquake ever recorded in Japan triggered a tsunami that swept over Japan's main island. The tsunami swept over the sea wall and flooded the nuclear power plant in Fukushima. This was very, very bad.
The power plant overheated, and radioactive material leaked out into the air and into the ocean.

WHY WAS IT A PROBLEM?

Depending on how radioactive something is, people might only be able to be around it for a few hours, a few minutes, or sometimes even a few seconds before getting very, very ill. So, how radioactive was it inside the Fukushima power plant after this tsunami? Well, that's just it – scientists weren't entirely sure!

WHAT DID THEY DO?

In the months that came after the disaster, robots trundled into the power plant buildings on their tracks and wheels to help scientists take a closer look, but they weren't built to deal with such danger!

They took readings of the temperature, oxygen levels, and radioactivity, but they weren't able to do much else! They couldn't fix anything inside the power plant, they couldn't clean up any of the radioactive material, and they couldn't make it safer for humans to go inside.

Because of all the radiation, and how far away people needed to stay to be safe, the robots would also lose contact with their human operators. There is even a section of the power plant known as the "robot graveyard" where these brave little bots went.

When the disaster happened in 2011, there weren't enough robots around that were advanced enough to properly help. This inspired some scientists to create the Darpa Robotics Challenge – a competition to design and build bigger, better, faster, and stronger semi-autonomous disaster robots that can work with humans to save humans.

Twenty-three teams from around the world competed in the finals where they sent their robots out into a disaster-zone obstacle course. The robots had an hour to move around the area and complete tasks like driving a car, walking up steps, clearing a path or walking over rubble, drilling a hole in a wall, and turning a valve.

You might be thinking - that sounds easy! Walking up steps? Turning a valve? Easy peasy.

Well, doing it yourself is one thing, but getting a robot to do it is a lot more complicated!

Twenty-five years before the Fukushima nuclear disaster, in April 1986, there was another nuclear disaster. This one happened in Ukraine at the Chernobyl nuclear power plant. If robots weren't ready for the nuclear disaster in Fukushima, they really weren't ready for the disaster in Chernobyl.

CHERNOBYL DISASTER

A huge explosion at the power plant released radiation into the atmosphere. So much radiation was released that it's still not safe to go there, even now.

WHAT DID THEY DO?

After the explosion, disaster teams sent robots into the danger zone, but the radiation levels were so high that these robots started going wrong and completely breaking down. If that's what was happening to the robots, just imagine how dangerous it was for humans.

In 2016, 30 years after the explosion, a huge structure called the **New Safe Confinement (NSC)** was built over the most dangerous part of the power plant. "Safe" might make you think it's, well, safe, but you'd be mistaken.

There is still almost 30 tonnes (33 tons) of radioactive dust inside the **NSC**, and if this dust gets on anything or anyone who ventures inside, it could easily escape and cause some serious damage.

SPOT

One robot that has already ventured inside the NSC is a quadruped robotic dog called Spot. Spot's four legs are perfect for moving around this dangerous and dusty disaster zone. Wheels and tracks would disturb the dust and move it around all over the place. Spot's tiny feet only leave tiny footprints, and tiny footprints mean less radioactive dust is getting shaken up.

Scientists learned a lot about robots after the Fukushima disaster in 2011. In 2024, scientists used a remote-controlled robot to collect some radioactive fuel from the Fukushima power plant for the first time ever, and scientists have been very careful with how much radiation the Chernobyl robots are exposed to. The only thing worse than one robot graveyard is two of them!

Hopefully, a nuclear disaster will never happen again, but if it does, at least we know the scientists and their robots are ready.

Chapter 6

ROBOTS ON A SPACE QUEST

You know somewhere else that's dangerous for humans to explore? **SPACE!**

FUN FACT: FIRST TRIP TO SPACE

Yuri Gagarin from the Soviet Union was the first person to ever fly to space. He stayed in his rocket, Vostok 1, and circled our little blue planet at an eye-watering 27,400 kilometers per hour (around 17,025 miles per hour).

Since then, humans just cannot get enough. We have sent hángtiān yuán (or taikonauts) from China, astronauts from the USA and Europe, and cosmonauts from Russia up into space to fly amongst the stars. Humans love space so much that the Tiangong space station and the Internation Space Station that are floating around Earth always have people living and working on board.

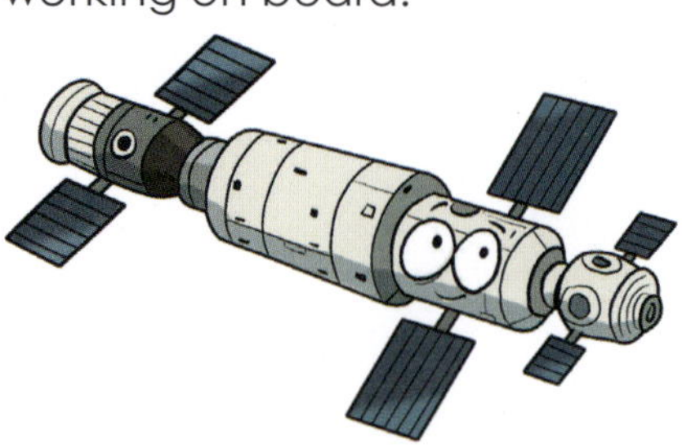

International Space Station

Tiangong Space Station

With all those twinkling stars and glittering moons, it might seem magical, or maybe even peaceful. But working in space can be very dangerous. One wrong move and it could be bye-bye brains. Literally!

Scientists up in space have a lot to think about all the time. There are a lot of different jobs to do every day, and some of these can be very dangerous.

SPACE ROBOTS

XIANG HANG ROBOT

Humans up in space are making use of robots all the time. People working on the Tiangong space station orbiting Earth have been getting help from a little space robot assistant called Xiao Hang.

Xiao Hang can move around in microgravity and take photos. Xiao Hang is quite a simple little bot, but it has been very important in helping scientists understand how humans and robots can work together in space.

You've heard of taikonauts, cosmonauts, and astronauts, but did you know there's another type of –naut?

MEET ROBONAUT!

Robonaut is a humanoid robot built by the USA's National Aeronautics and Space Administration (NASA), and in 2011, Robonaut2 became the first ever humanoid robot in space. With its dainty little hands, Robonaut can use the same tools as humans, which makes it perfect for doing fiddly, delicate, and complicated jobs up in space that so far only people have been able to do.

Scientists aren't planning for humanoid robots to replace our human space explorers, though. They actually hope that robots and humans will be able to work alongside each other, just like they are already with robots like little Xiao Hang!

Robonaut might one day be able to take over and automate simple, repetitive, boring, or dangerous jobs on places like the International Space Station, so the humans on board can focus on exploring new worlds or working on scientific experiments.

While Robonaut might be perfect for some tasks in space, other jobs need something a little bigger and a LOT stronger.

When something with a bit more muscle is needed, robotic arms are perfect for the job. The Tiangong space station has two robotic arms. These arms can be controlled from inside the station and can grab, crawl, and help their human teammates make repairs to the outside of the station.

CANADARM2

Canadarm2 is attached to the outside of the International Space Station and is a MASSIVE 17 meters (55 feet) long!

It has two handy little robotic hands called Latching End Effectors, and scientists on Earth or in space can use these to make repairs to the space station, move around supplies, equipment, and astronauts, and even catch spaceships and attach them to the space station.

DEXTRE

Dextre is a two-armed robot that can be attached to the end of Canadarm2. Each of its arms can move up and down, side to side, and rotate all the way around. This means Dextre can actually move in ways that a human arm can't! Dextre has built in cameras, lights, and tools and can be controlled from Earth, all while the crew on the International Space Station are asleep! This robot is so skilled that it can handle gear as small as a toaster or as large as a refrigerator, and is the only robot ever to have repaired itself in space!

So, there are lots of robots that are great for working with humans in space, but sometimes we need robots that can be a little more independent.

There might be humans living and working on the space stations orbiting our planet, but to really see what's out there we need robots that go where we can't follow them.

Landers and rovers are robotic spacecraft that are built to explore other worlds – this might be our Moon, our red neighbor Mars, or even asteroids (the small chunks of rock that orbit our Sun).

Sure, humans have been to the Moon before, but they have to come back eventually! Robots can stay there a lot longer than any humans could.

LANDERS

Landers are spacecraft that are built to land (come on, you could have guessed that, right?!). Rather than crashing into their target with impact (that would be an impact probe!), landers make a soft landing.

Landers usually can't move around, so they can only really take readings or photos of whatever is around them.

ROVERS

If landers can land, rovers can rove! These robots have wheels that are designed especially to be able to travel over the rough surface of the Moon and Mars. Rovers can explore without being controlled by a human, and they usually have cameras and sensors that they use to tell us exactly what they're finding, seeing, and measuring. For us Earthlings, they're a bit like our very own out-of-this-world pen pals!

Lots of humans and lots of robots have been to the Moon, but all of these people and spacecraft have always landed on the side of the Moon that faces Earth. In 2019, China did something AMAZING that had never been done before – they made the first ever landing on the far side of the Moon!

This landing was part of the China National Space Administration's (CNSA) Chang'e 4 mission, and Yutu-2 is the brave little lunar rover that's part of it.

VISITING THE MOON

YUTU-2

Yutu-2 is about the size of a small car and is powered by the Sun. It has solar panels that soak up the Sun's energy and use it to charge up its batteries to move around. Handy for a place where there are no power outlets!

Yutu-2 explores places that have never been seen before and takes photos that it sends back to the scientists on Earth. Like any good robot, it's fitted with special tools and sensors that it uses to study the dirt and rocks on the Moon's surface. It can even look below the ground to find out more about what's inside the Moon. Humans haven't been to the Moon in over 50 years, and no human has ever gone to the far side of the Moon, so Yutu-2 is a bit like a robot explorer and robot scientist all rolled into one little rover.

Yutu-2 was only supposed to last three months, but it has been working for years! In fact, it ended up breaking records, becoming the rover that has worked on the Moon's surface for the longest!

Yutu-2 might be completing its mission alone, but there have been plenty of other rovers on the surface of the Moon.

CHANG'E 6 ROVER

Jinchan is CNSA's Chang'e 6 rover and it is TINY, weighing only 5 kilograms (11 pounds). It landed on the far side of the Moon in 2024 and, using its four tiny wheels, rolled out in search of interesting samples to bring back to Earth.

UNFORTUNATELY, JINCHAN AND YUTU-2 NEVER MET, BUT I'M SURE THEY'D BE GREAT FRIENDS!

Sojourner, Spirit, Opportunity, Curiosity, and Perseverance aren't the members of a cool new boyband – they're the names of NASA's different Mars rovers! Starting with Sojourner all the way back in 1997, NASA has sent five different rovers to Mars. While orbiters take photos as they orbit Mars, and landers take photos and collect data from their landing spots, Mars rovers are like the rovers on the Moon – they specialize in moving around to different spots, collecting information as they go. Using their onboard tools, rovers can study the different chemicals in the different rocks on Mars and teach human scientists back on Earth all about how the environments on Mars changed these rocks over time.

1997 - SOJOURNER

Sojourner landed in 1997 and was the first robot with wheels to explore Mars. Sojourner sent back more than 550 photos of Mars. With the information Sojourner collected, scientists learned that Mars used to be a lot warmer and a lot wetter!

2004 - SPIRIT AND OPPORTUNITY

Spirit and Opportunity are identical rovers that arrived on the red planet in 2004. It was their mission to find any evidence of water on Mars.

2012 - CURIOSITY

Curiosity landed on Mars in 2012 and is as curious as its name suggests! Its mission is to find out whether there were ever tiny living things on Mars. Curiosity uses a special drill to make holes in rocks and has seventeen cameras for taking photos of its adventures. It's been exploring Mars for thirteen years and has traveled over thirty-four kilometers (twenty-one miles). A year after it landed on Mars, it sang itself Happy Birthday!

2021 - PERSEVERANCE

Perseverance touched down in 2021 and is looking for signs of life on Mars. Could humans ever go to Mars, and could they survive there? It's Perseverance's job to find out!

2021 - ZHURONG

Perseverance wasn't the only rover to land on Mars in 2021. In 2021, Zhurong became the first rover from China to land on Mars. It's powered by fold-out solar panels and has cameras that sit on a very tall mast that it uses to take photos and help it find its way around the planet.

Zhurong is part of China's Tianwen-1 mission, and this mission is a great example of teamwork and how scientists around the world can work together to solve some big questions!

Getting something off Earth, into space, and then safely back down to Mars isn't easy. It's important for scientists to know exactly where the spacecraft is at all times just in case something goes wrong. The European Space Agency (ESA) has stations all around the world that can pick up signals from space. ESA and CNSA worked together to use these stations to track Tianwen-1 through space and make sure it landed on Mars with no problems.

When Zhurong made it to Mars, it had some pretty important jobs to do. Scientists from space teams in France and Austria helped to design and build the tools that Zhurong is using to explore Mars.

One of these tools is something called LIBS. This stands for Laser Induced Breakdown Spectroscopy. Zhurong uses LIBS to zap rocks and soil on Mars with lasers. This creates a teeny, tiny explosion that turns part of the rock into a hot, glowing gas called plasma. Scientists can study the light that comes off this plasma to find out what the rock is made of.
Pretty impressive stuff!

Since its big landing in 2021, Zhurong has been making waves in the world of space exploration. Zhurong shot radio waves down under the surface of Mars and studied the way these waves reflected back. Using these waves, it found sloping layers of sand—the very first evidence of ancient beaches on Mars!

Things can be difficult when we work alone, but when we work together, we can achieve a lot more!

Designing robots that can survive on a planet like Mars isn't easy. Huge dust storms can last for days, weeks, or even months, blocking out sunlight and making it difficult to see anything. The temperature can also swing between a nice, warm 20°C (70°F) and an icy, freezing, teeth-chattering, and absolutely bone-chilling -153°C (-225°F).

That's why the Mars Society, a group of scientists who want to get humans to Mars, created the International University Rover Challenge.

INTERNATIONAL UNIVERSITY ROVER CHALLENGE

The University Rover Challenge is a competition for college students that's held every year in the Mars-like desert of southern Utah in the USA. The competition challenges teams of students to design and build the next generation of Mars rovers that might one day be sent to Mars and, like Zhurong, make some dizzying discoveries that could get humans one step closer to living on another planet!

Another team of scientists working to get us to Mars is the Resilient ExtraTerrestrial Habitats institute, but you can call them RETHi! RETHi is using everything we've learned about Mars to design and build deep space human habitats.

Scientists aren't sure how long it will take to get humans to Mars, so we need to build somewhere that's ready and waiting for us when we do arrive.

But wait, how can we build a habitat on Mars before any humans arrive? **You guessed it – robots!** Because humans won't always be there to lend a helping hand, these robots need to work autonomously.

RETHI

RETHi are designing end-effectors that can change their shape to hold different objects in different ways, just like human hands. Handy! The next step is making sure the robots can recognize different objects and know exactly how to grip and move them using these fancy, adaptable end-effectors. Once the robots have got a grip on this, scientists hope they'll be able to build, maintain, and repair a new Martian home for us!

ONE SMALL STEP FOR ROBOTS, ONE GIANT LEAP FOR HUMANKIND!

Autonomous robots are the perfect machines for building habitats in space, but they're also great for exploring space and showing us all the places we can't get to ourselves.

So far, humans haven't made it farther than the Moon, and we're still trying to get to Mars, so humans reaching outer space is still a long way off.

SPACE PROBES

Space probes are a bit like robotic spaceships. They're usually very small and have no one inside. In 2024, a little robotic space probe followed pre-programmed instructions and flew past the Sun, (yes, THE Sun!) closer than any human-made object ever before, reaching temperatures of 1,000°C (1,832°F)!

Just think how hot and sweaty you feel on a warm, summer's day on Earth. Humans would never be able to get that close to the Sun without burning up, boiling, or being completely vaporized! Thanks to these space bots, humans are reaching new heights and exploring completely uncharted territory.

VOYAGER 1 AND 2

Voyager 1 and Voyager 2 are identical probes that were launched by NASA all the way back in 1977 and they've been zooming through space ever since! The Voyagers (that's what their friends call them) haven't stopped at all in all of that time – not even once!

The Voyagers communicate with scientists back on Earth using something called the Deep Space Network.

This is a huge system of **GIANT** and **SUPER POWERFUL** radio antennas that listen to signals from spacecraft and send messages back to them. Because of how very, very far away the Voyagers are from Earth, these messages can take hours or even DAYS to come in, so the probes follow pre-programmed instructions on their onboard computers to carry out their tasks and make decisions.

VOYAGERS' FIRST MISSION

Their first mission was to check out our GIANT planetary neighbors Jupiter and Saturn.

FINDINGS

They found active volcanoes on Jupiter's moon Io and sent back detailed photos of Saturn's rings. And now they're on a one-way mission to go far, far away.

Voyager 1 is over 24 billion kilometers (15 billion miles) away, and Voyager 2 is over 20 billion kilometers (13 billion miles) away. Not bad for a couple of 50-year-old robots!

The future of space robots looks bright, and it's not just because we're looking at the Sun! (Definitely do not look at the Sun! We're not looking at the Sun, and neither should you!) If you've been paying attention, you'll know robots are really changing the world, or should we say, the universe, and there's no plan for them to slow down any time soon. Scientists are still working on ways to bring out bigger, better, and smarter robots that we can send to space.

TAIKOBOT

One of these fancy future robots is a humanoid robot space assistant called Taikobot. Taikobot has been designed by scientists in China and will hopefully one day be heading to the Tiangong space station as a new member of the team.

Taikobot has two arms, two hands, sensors, and cameras that it can use to move equipment, hold and control tools, and do simple and repetitive jobs to help Hángtiān yuán around the station. Humans in space need beds, toilets, food, and lots of other complicated things. Taikobot only needs solar energy to survive.

COULD ROBOT SPACE ASSISTANTS BE THE FUTURE?

ASTROBEE

A less-human-looking robot assistant is NASA's Astrobee. You might think Astrobee would look like a bee, but it's actually made up of three cubed-shaped robots. It uses electric fans to push it through the air, cameras and sensors to help it "see", and a special arm that lets it grasp the station's handrails to save energy or to grab and hold items.

Astrobee can work on its own or be controlled remotely, and scientists hope it will one day take on jobs like moving cargo around the station, leaving the very important astronauts to do the very important jobs only humans can do.

Maybe one day in the future we'll have smart robot space assistants that have whole personalities. They might control our spacecraft, make suggestions on missions and experiments, and use artificial intelligence and machine learning to adapt to what's happening around them.

Chapter 7

ROBOTS IN THE DEEP

Thanks to some incredible spacecraft and robots, and the super-brainy scientists who built them, we know an awful lot about space. You might think there's still a lot to explore, and there is (in case you didn't already know, space is MASSIVE), but there's somewhere else a lot closer to home that holds just as many mysteries...

70% of our Earth's surface is covered by oceans, but over 80% of them are completely unexplored! Who knows what mysteries are lurking in their depths... Some scientists even believe that we know more about the surface of the Moon and Mars than we do about the ocean floor on our own planet!

Animals and plants in the ocean can be very delicate. The last thing scientists want to do is send down a big, clumsy, hulking robot, with swinging manipulators and end-effectors. This could cause some serious damage!

Water is also heavy, and the farther down you go, the more water there is on top of you. This water pushes

down

and **down**

and **down**

and creates more and more pressure. The pressure can be so strong that it can crush big, metal robots and even people!

The ocean can also be very dark and unpredictable.

The ocean can also be very dark and unpredictable. The ocean is full of surprises, like deep cracks and crevices, volcanic vents, and spiky coral reefs that could make it impossible for rigid, roaming robots to explore the ocean surface.

If only there were something different, something softer perhaps? Well, do I have news for you! There is something softer. Welcome to the wonderful world of...

SOFT ROBOTICS!

Usually, robots are made from HARD materials like metal and plastic. And they're not just hard on the outside, either – their insides are hard, too! These robots are powered by hard batteries and hard motors, and they have hard manipulators and hard end-effectors.

Nature is great at designing soft and squidgy creatures that can survive in the ocean. These creatures aren't stiff and rigid and made of hard, clunky metal, or plastic. And they don't get squashed by the crushing pressure of the ocean either.

BONUS! If you can't beat them, join them, and that's exactly what some bright-spark brainboxes have been doing!

WHAT IS SOFT ROBOTICS?

Soft robotics is the design, control, and creation of robots that use soft, flexible materials instead of hard, rigid ones. Soft roboticists take inspiration from nature to create robots that are soft and flexible, just like an animal!

Sometimes they might even look a bit like an animal, too! There are lots of things that hard, rigid robots are great for, but soft robots are perfect for exploring our oceans.

They're lighter than rigid robots and can easily glide through water, just like a jellyfish or an octopus, using less energy to push them forward. They're also more flexible and can change their shape to make it easier to deal with the EXTREME PRESSURE down at the bottom of the ocean. They can bend, stretch, squeeze, and squish into tight spaces like underwater caves, too. These little softies also have a very soft touch. Their soft arms and grippers can gently poke, prod, move, and carefully collect things from the ocean floor, all without causing any damage.

WHILE WE'RE HERE AT THE BOTTOM OF THE OCEAN, WE MIGHT AS WELL TAKE A LOOK AROUND!

DEEPSTALK

DeepStalk is a soft, fleshy robot inspired by the humble sea snail. It has been designed by scientists at Zhejiang University in China and has transformed the world of soft robotics thanks to the way it sees and moves!

DeepStalk has tentacles just like a sea snail, but instead of having eyes at the end of each tentacle, it has cameras! And believe it or not, these tentacles can actually move!

FUN FACT: SEA SNAILS HAVE TENTACLES!

You're probably imagining the tentacles of an octopus. Well, stop imagining! Sea snails have very different tentacles. These tentacles are more like eyestalks, and instead of using them to move around, they use them to "see" the world around them.

When you need to move a part of your body, you flex your muscles. They go from being r e l a x e d to being contracted. When your muscles are relaxed, they might feel soft and flabby, but when they're contracted, they might feel rock solid.

Robots don't have muscles, but scientists have found a way to give soft robots like DeepStalk fake muscles by using something called shape memory alloys.

Shape memory alloys, or SMAs, remember shapes! They can be put into one position when they're cold and then return to their "remembered" shape when they're heated up.

DeepStalk uses SMAs to bend and then straighten its eyestalks. Scientists hope DeepStalk will one day be able to track things underwater by using its moveable eyestalks by using its moveable eyestalks to look at things moving around it.

Think this sounds smart? You're right! These are called smart materials.

WHAT ARE SMART MATERIALS?

Smart materials are materials that can be changed to be one way, and then changed back again using heat, light, pressure, magnets, or electricity. Smart materials might change shape, like the SMAs used in DeepStalk, or even change color!

IMAGINE THIS:

Just imagine being able to change the color of your clothes with just a click of your fingers. How fancy!

Scientists at Zhejiang University have yet another soft robot up their sleeves, ready to take on the ocean and explore its murky depths with the help of some very smart materials.

ROBOTIC FISH

This robot is shaped like a fish, and it even has fins and a tail. It uses SMAs that, when powered by a battery, make a "muscle" in its body bend and straighten, just like DeepStalk. This bending and straightening makes the robot's fins flap and flap, up and down, like the fins of a manta ray. These flapping fins propel the robotic fish through the water, faster than other swimming robots that have come before it.

Smart materials really are the future of robotics, and scientists at Beijing Jiaotong University in China have come up with a very clever way to make more and more smart materials – by using 3D printing,

WHAT IS 4D PRINTING?

3D printing is when you use a computer and a printer to create a 3D object by laying down lots of very thin layers that build up and up. 4D printing uses the same technique, but the thing you end up with is made from smart materials - by using 3D printing.

Science is all about...

TEAMWORK!

Teamwork is helping scientists come up with new and exciting robots all the time!

PROJECT: DEEP SEA CORAL ROBOTS

Dr David Gruber is a marine biologist. This means that he studies the things that live in our oceans. In 2014, Dr Gruber gave a talk about his work exploring deep sea coral reefs. He showed a video of some big, clunky, clumsy, and rigid robotic hands that he had used to collect samples of coral and sponges from the bottom of the ocean. It can be difficult to know if these living things will be fragile, brittle, hard, or soft.

FINDINGS

These little corals and sponges that Dr Gruber was interested in were very fragile, and these hard, rigid robotic hands were definitely not the right robots for the job! They were too big, too powerful, and were leaving a path of destruction in their wake.

Professor Robert Wood is a roboticist from Harvard University in the USA. Professor Wood is an expert in soft robotics, so when he saw this, he had an idea. Ding! Ding! Ding! Brilliant Idea Alert!

PROJECT: DEEP SEA SOFT ROBOTICS

Dr Gruber hadn't heard of soft robotics before, so he joined forces with Professor Wood and together they created a deep-sea soft robotics super dream team! They worked together to design some remote-controlled squishy robotic fingers, made mostly from rubber.

FINDINGS

These have transformed deep-sea exploration and saved ocean floors all over our planet from pesky rigid robots! Soft robots can grip and grasp a lot more gently and delicately, and these squishy fingers were able to collect coral and sponges without destroying the precious samples, or anything else for that matter!

Scientists can't know everything about everything, but when they work together, they can share what they know, make new discoveries, and solve more problems together.

You probably know that our oceans are full of fish, but did you know they're also full of trash?

They shouldn't be full of trash, but unfortunately lots of garbage has made its way into our seas. This is bad news for the plants and animals that call the oceans their home. Some animals get caught up and tangled in big bits of trash that can wrap around their bodies and bring an end to our poor fishy friends.

It's also bad news for us and the planet. Ocean trash can destroy delicate habitats and even make its way into the seafood we eat.

Luckily for us, and more luckily for ocean creatures big and small, scientists from around the world have been working hard to help our planet and clean up our oceans using soft robotics.

ENVIRONMENTAL ROBOTIC HELPERS

JELLYFISH-BOT

Jellyfish-Bot uses actuators that work like muscles to make it move. Electricity flows through Jellyfish-Bot to make its fins pulse up and down, making it gliiiiide and float through the ocean and move like a real jellyfish! As the robot moves through the water, it can collect ocean trash underneath its body and carry it all the way to the water's surface.

HOW DOES IT WORK?

When a jellyfish swims upward, it creates water currents around its body that can trap things in its path. Jellyfish-Bot works in the same way! This makes it the perfect robot for collecting trash from delicate places like coral reefs because it doesn't need to touch the trash it's picking up.

If it needs to, though, Jellyfish-Bot can use two of its six fins as grippers! It can even work with other Jellyfish-Bots to carry heavier loads. When robots work together, there's nothing they can't do!

Plastic is one of the worst types of trash. Over a long, long time, it breaks down into smaller and smaller pieces, but it never disappears completely. Some of these pieces are so so tiny that you can't see them without a microscope.

These super-small plastics are called microplastics, and they can end up anywhere and everywhere. They've been found on every part of our planet – from the ice on Antarctica to inside (yes, INSIDE!) fish living at the very bottom of the ocean, and even in the fresh water we drink; microplastics are impossible to escape.

Jellyfish-Bot isn't ready to hit the seven seas yet, but when it does it will be great at collecting big bits of trash, but it won't be able to collect these teeny tiny microplastics. After all, how do you collect something you can't even see?!

OCEAN TRASH REMOVAL SERVICE

Well, scientists at Sichuan University in China have found a way to collect microplastics, and it involves tiny soft robotic fish! These robots are only around 1 centimeter (0.4 inches) long, but they are fast.

HOW DO THEY WORK?

They are made of smart materials, so when a laser is pointed at the robot's tail, the material bends. When the laser is shone again and again, its tail bends from side to side, making it swim forward! Real fish accidentally gobble up microplastics all the time, but these robotic fish aren't hungry for plastic. Instead, the microplastics stick to their bodies as they swim on by.

Right now, these little fish can only collect microplastics from the ocean surface, but scientists hope they will one day be able to send these little bots deeper, all the way to the ocean floor.

Not all robots in the ocean are soft, but that doesn't mean they're not stillpretty smart and pretty cool. And they are helping us and the planet in some important and interesting ways!

ALGARAY

AlgaRay is a robot that collects a type of seaweed called Sargassum that's causing some BIG problems in the Caribbean and the Gulf of Mexico. While it's in the sea, Sargassum does a good job of providing a place for fish to live. The problems begin when piles and piles of it wash up on beaches. The seaweed can clog pipes and smother plants and animals. And when it starts to rot, it smells REALLY BAD.

HOW DOES IT WORK?

AlgaRay glides along the ocean surface, picking up Sargassum before it gets too close to the beach. Then, this clever robot dives 200 meters underwater and drops the seaweed, letting it sink to the ocean floor where it belongs.

Scientists hope that one day AlgaRay will be completely autonomous and able to patrol the ocean's surface around the clock. Busy bots are happy bots! Other robots on a mission to clean up our oceans are Clearbot's autonomous, solar-powered, robotic boats.

CLEARBOT

Clearbot was started as a university project by students at the University of Hong Kong, China in 2020, and now its boats are cleaning up rivers, lakes, and oceans in India, Hong Kong (China), and Thailand. The boats can be set to work on their own or controlled from anywhere in the world!

HOW DOES IT WORK?

Clearbot's boats are like garbage trucks for water. They collect garbage through a gap in their front. All the trash that's been collected moves up a conveyor belt before being safely stowed away in a basket in the middle of the boat.

Cleaning up the ocean can be dangerous, but Clearbot's mission is to make the world a cleaner and safer place while keeping humans safe, too!

The ocean can be a dangerous place. Sometimes, when a job is too dangerous for a human diver, we need to send in a robot to take our place.

AUVs and ROVs are both types of underwater robots that we can use to explore the deep, dark world of the deep, dark ocean floor.

AUVS

AUVs are autonomous underwater vehicles. These are sometimes called robot submarines or autosubs. AUVs are like robot investigators. They're sent down into the deep ocean to complete underwater missions, like finding and mapping submerged shipwrecks. Once their mission is completed, they return to the surface by following pre-programmed instructions that take them to a specific place.

Ocean gliders are a type of AUV. They look a bit like underwater rockets and can be sent on missions that take days, weeks, or sometimes even months! They have sensors that can collect information from places it would be too dangerous to send a human diver.

ROVS AND ROUVS

ROVs are remotely operated vehicles. They might sometimes be called ROUVs, which stands for remotely operated underwater vehicles. They're similar to AUVs, but instead of being automated, they're remote-controlled. They're usually attached to a ship by cables that carry signals between the human operator and the ROV.

ROVs might have a video camera, lights, and robotic arms that can be used to make underwater repairs, collect items from the bottom of the sea, or to attach lifting hooks to larger objects that can be collected by bigger and stronger machines.

As soft robotics and smart materials become better and better, more and more AUVs and ROVs will be softer and smarter, and a whole new generation of underwater robots will be ready to explore our oceans for us.

Chapter 8

DR. ROBOT WILL SEE YOU NOW

Hospitals are pretty gross places. There's a lot of snot and blood and people being sick everywhere. Nobody wants to go to hospital, and being a doctor can be a difficult job.

Luckily, robots don't care about all that gross human stuff. They never get sick or stressed. And it turns out they can be really great at healing humans.

ROBOTS IN HOSPITALS

Robots are already used in lots of places around hospitals right now. If you were thinking robots could be used in surgery... you are right! If you were thinking robots could be used to discover diseases in the body... you are right! If you were thinking doctors might secretly be robots with fake skin and hair... actually, you'd be wrong, we're pretty sure doctors are human.

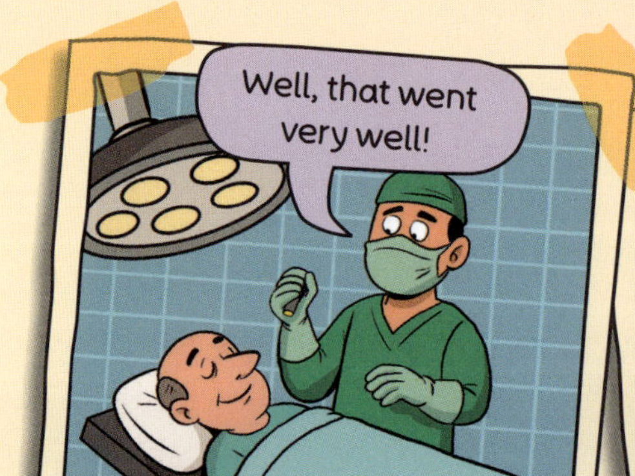

Robots are used to save lives every day, working alongside doctors and surgeons. However, they also help in other ways, such as cleaning.

ROBOT CLEANERS

Cleaning might not sound exciting, but keeping things clean in a hospital can be the difference between life and death. A clean room means no germs, which means healthy people. **So, scrub, robots, scrub!**

ROBOT HELPERS

Some robots are programmed to carry things around the hospital. These robots take meals (yum!), bed sheets (yawn) and human waste (ew, poo!) where they need to be. This keeps the whole hospital working smoothly.

Right now, humans and robots work together. But in the future, the robots might do all of this on their own. They may do surgery without humans controlling them. They could also test medicines in laboratories on their own. We might even be talking to robots about our illness in the future, so they can use their big robot brains to figure out what is making us sick.

DO YOU KNOW WHAT SURGERY IS?

It is when someone (called a surgeon) cuts a person (called a patient) open to look inside the body and fix any problems.

(Psst, don't worry – surgery isn't painful. People are given special medicine which means they don't feel a thing.)

Surgery saves millions of lives. You might think it is weird that we can make an injured person feel better by cutting them up. Well, it's about to get even weirder...

Robots are doing surgery right now. These robo-surgeons can be controlled or programmed by humans to do very tricky tasks. It's like playing a video game, but on super hard mode where you only have one life (or rather, someone else's life).

ROBODOC

When it comes to hip surgeries, there's nobody better than ROBODOC. In 1992, it became the first robot to do surgery on a human (with help from surgeons, of course). ROBODOC uses a computerized 3D planning system. This means it knows the exact movements to make to perform an almost-perfect surgery. Once the pre-programming is completed by humans, ROBODOC is ready to go. It has done thousands of surgeries since, all over the world.

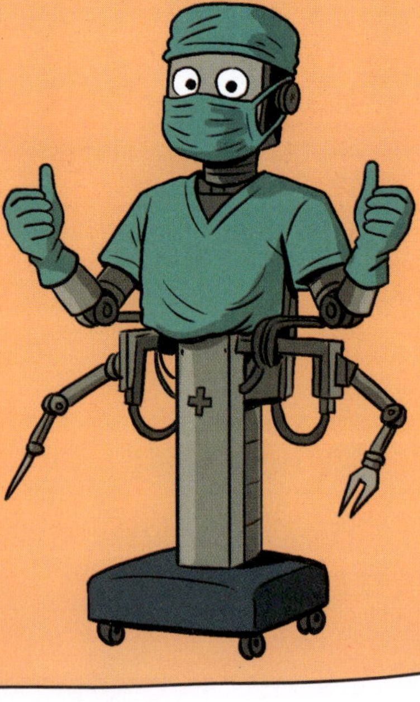

DA VINCI

But if you don't want to travel the world, then you should meet da Vinci. Surgeons can control da Vinci from far away to do surgery. So, a surgeon can be in a different building in a whole different city and save a person's life without even meeting them! They control da Vinci using a special computer with joysticks, and use this robot to make smaller, more careful cuts that would be impossible for humans. This means sick people recover faster from surgery, and feel better weeks earlier than usual.

NEUROARM

There's another robot that is willing to lend a hand in surgeries. Actually, it is willing to lend a whole arm: meet NeuroArm. This robot helps with brain surgeries. Just like da Vinci, NeuroArm can be controlled by a surgeon who is very far away.

One of the differences is that NeuroArm works in an MRI machine. There are two things you need to know about MRI machines: firstly, they help doctors see inside brains. Secondly, they have giant magnets inside so you can't put anything metal nearby. So, no robots made of steel are allowed.

So why don't the magnets make NeuroArm flail around like it's being electrocuted at a concert? Well, NeuroArm isn't made of magnetic metals. The arm is steady as a rock, which is pretty important when you are cutting open something as squishy and important as a brain. NeuroArm sends images, sounds, and even a sense of touch to the surgeon who is controlling it.

So, if you find yourself in hospital and need surgery, you might be thanking a robot for saving your life. **Thank you robots!**

But don't forget, it takes a lot of clever people working together to create these robots, such as scientists, doctors, and engineers. **Thank you, clever people!**

That's better! Hopefully you will never have to have surgery, anyway!

Cutting people open is always the last thing a doctor wants to do. It's much better to prevent diseases or treat them without surgery. Robots are getting involved in this, too.

"Diagnostic" is a word that means working out what illness a person has. So, diagnostic robots find out what diseases people have as early as possible. And the quicker we find out what is wrong with someone, the easier it is to make them better.

PROBLEMS

When doctors want to find out what is wrong with someone's gut, they grab a very long tube with a tiny camera on the end and stick it down the patient's throat. Or sometimes the camera goes up the patient's bum. This isn't much fun at all.

SOLUTION?

Capsule robots give doctors the ability to look for diseases without needing to stick anything down anyone's throat. These robots are small, usually only a few millimeters big. This is about the size of a pill. When they are swallowed, they can explore the whole digestive tract – everything from your mouth to your bum, including your throat, stomach, intestines, and colon.

It is made of a special type of plastic which is safe for the human body but cannot be digested.

But what if doctors need to look for diseases that aren't in the digestive tract? Well, there are lots of other types of diagnostic robots.

Some robots use ultrasound to find diseases in people without looking inside them. Ultrasound means using sound to create a picture. How weird is that?!

This is useful if you want to look inside the body without putting anything inside the body. Ultrasound is used to check on babies when they are still in their mother's body. It is also used for looking at hearts, or looking at the stiff, creaky joints of old people.

1 First, a type of gel is put on the body part.

2 Once it is all nice and messy, it's time for the robots to join in. Using a robot arm, the machine scans the body part.

3 It can then tell the patient or the doctor what is going on inside, and what might be wrong.

Finding diseases is all well and good, but...

WHAT ROBOTS ACTUALLY TREAT DISEASES?

Cancer is a serious disease. There are lots of different types of cancer depending on which part of the body has the disease. Most types of cancer make growths appear inside the body, which cause damage. These growths are called tumors.

There are a few ways to get rid of these tumors. One way is to blast them with a powerful type of energy called radiation. But there's a problem – while radiation is bad news for tumors, it is also bad news for the rest of the body as well. So, doctors have to be very careful with using radiation.

CYBERKNIFE

A robot called CyberKnife is ready to help. Although CyberKnife might sound like a supervillain's name, this robot's real job is getting rid of tumors caused by cancer.

Don't worry, this robot doesn't really have a knife. It just has a deadly beam of radiation! Yay!

Using cameras and sensors, the robot targets the exact place where the tumor is. It can even track the movements of a person, so if they breathe or change position, CyberKnife moves its beam, too.

With CyberKnife, people with cancer only need a few visits before their tumor is destroyed, all without surgery.

Not all diseases can be cured, though. And sometimes, humans just need a bit of comforting, especially when they are dealing with these diseases. But most robots are just cold, metal arms, or big, humming boxes with lights on. That's not very comforting...

Well, good news: friendly, cuddly robots do exist.

CUDDLY ROBOTS

These lovable robots can be furry and shaped to look like baby animals. If you pet them, they can wiggle and makes noises. If you say their name, they can turn towards you.

Friendly robots and pet robots are made to be used by all sorts of people. These bots have been used to comfort older people with brain diseases. They're also used to help children who find it difficult to talk and express their feelings.

If someone has a brain injury, it can take months or years for them to relearn how to move and use parts of their body. One type of brain injury is called a stroke. If someone has had a stroke, they might lose the ability to control their arms or legs properly.

There are two types of robots that can help a person recovering from injuries to the brain. The first one is called an exoskeleton.

"What?? What is it going to do to my skeleton??" you might say. Calm down, it's scarier than it sounds.

TYPE 1: EXOSKELETON

Exoskeleton just means something hard covering the body, and that's exactly what these robots do. They fit over the body part, and the person then exercises. The robot is tough to move, which makes the exercise harder and builds the muscles up. The exoskeletons can also be linked to a game on a screen. The player must do the exercises to score points and complete objectives in the game.

The other type is end-effector robots.

TYPE 2: END-EFFECTOR ROBOTS

This just means the robot has a handle or controller which the person grabs onto when doing the exercises. Just like exoskeletons, the end-effector robots use exercise to play games on a screen.

Exoskeleton robots can also be soft and wearable, like clothes. These soft exosuits use actuators. Remember, you can think of actuators like the muscles of a robot.

With these actuators, soft exosuits can help a human move their legs, arms, shoulders, or any other body part. This could make their movements more powerful, or it could mean they wouldn't get tired as quickly.

There are two main types of actuators used by soft exosuits.

TYPE 1:

The first are cables, which are wound up and down using electric motors.

TYPE 2:

The second type use air that has been squished into a tank. When the air is released, it forces parts of the soft exosuit to move.

For people with injuries, soft exosuits could be life changing. Serious injuries to the spine or brain can damage nerve cells – the cells that tell body parts to move. Other diseases can affect muscles. In both of these cases, these people would find it hard to move. But a comfortable soft exosuit would give them the power they need to move around freely.

These soft exosuits are still in the testing stage, so they aren't actually being used in the real world. But imagine one day owning an exosuit of your own.

You might be wondering about people who weren't born with all their arms and legs, or who have lost some. And you'd be right – exosuits are no good for them. But robotic bionic limbs are.

ROBOTIC BIONIC LIMBS

WHAT ARE THEY?

Bionic limbs are arms and legs made of strong, light materials like carbon fiber. Some are strapped to the body, and some are fixed to the body using surgery. Robotic bionic limbs use sensors to measure electrical signals that come from the brain. They then use these signals to move the limb. So, if a person without legs thinks "I want to step forward", it sends those signals to the robotic limb, which then moves.

HOW DO THEY WORK?

Robotic limbs use sensors and robotic controllers to automatically help the person use the limb. For example, this can help a person walk around obstacles. Some limbs also use AI, so that the machine learns the more the person uses it.

Robotic limbs are very expensive right now. But if they get cheaper in the future, more people might be able to use them.

The future of robots is sometimes called "black technology". It means black in the same way the night is dark and we can't see everything. Black technology can mean future technology that will work in ways we don't yet understand. It can also mean real technology that exists today that is really, really complicated so most people don't understand it.

So, you can think of black technology as futuristic technology. And when it comes to robots that cure diseases and fix injuries, black technology is actually quite bright and exciting!

LET'S LOOK AT SOME BLACK TECHNOLOGY:

WORD BLOCKS: TELESURGERY

Telephone - something that can help you speak to people from anywhere.

Television - something that allows you to watch stuff from all over the world.

Telesurgery - so this means you can do surgery from very far away.

JINGFENG POROUS ROBOT SYSTEM

The Jingfeng porous robot system in China is one of these long-range robots. Surgeons use it with remote controls. Like the da Vinci, the surgeon could control the robot from very far away. This was the first long-range robot surgeon in China to pass important tests designed to make sure it is safe.

SO, HOW FAR AWAY CAN THE SURGEON BE FROM THE ROBOT?

The biggest distance so far has been 8264 kilometers (5135 miles)! It was all the way from London, England to Beijing, China.

So, this is an example of very complicated technology that exists today. But what about future technology that is still being built?

LET'S TALK ABOUT NANOBOTS.

You've already read about capsule robots, which are only a few millimeters big. Well, remember nanobots? Nanobots are even smaller than capsule robots. Nanobots can be 100 times thinner than a single human hair. Be careful not to lose them – it'll take forever to find them again!

The goal of some nanobots is not just to find diseases or injuries, but to actually treat the problem. During testing, nanobots could reach deeper areas than any other robot or human surgeon, which means there are all sorts of exciting and helpful things they could do. They've already been used to get rid of clots in blood vessels.

Nanobots can be remote controlled. They move through the body in all sorts of ways, including using magnets. Once they reach the target, they can find diseases, release medicine, or do surgery. Scientists having been building tiny magnetic-controlled drills that the nanobots can use as a type of surgical knife.

But in the future, these nanobots might have competition. They aren't the only robot getting ready to plunge into the gross depths of the human body.

INVENTION

Scientists at the Chinese University of Hong Kong, China, and Harbin Institute of Technology are working on slime robots. Even though these wibbly wobbly robots look like something that crawled out of the toilet, they are actually very high tech and ready for action.

WHAT DO THEY DO?

Slime robots are controlled using magnets. They can squeeze themselves through tight spaces and even grab onto things. Slime robots can change shape, and are sometimes more watery like a liquid, and other times more firm like a (squidgy) solid. They can also heal themselves!

THE FUTURE OF SLIME ROBOTS

One day, slime robots may be used inside human bodies. They would be able to swallow and carry harmful things, check for diseases, deliver medicine, and carry out surgery. Hopefully by then they will look less gross, though.

Chapter 9

THE FUTURE IS ROBOTIC

From black technology to soft robotics, smart materials, and biomimicry, the future of robotics is very exciting indeed. Even now, big-brained scientists are still making epic discoveries every single day that are changing our lives and changing the world.

Some people are afraid that humans might be replaced by robots one day. Robots that steal our friends, steal our jobs, and steal our homes. Robots that are so clever they outsmart even their creators. Robots that are cleverer than you, me, and even the cleverest, most intelligent scientists on our planet.

Of course, scientists are always trying to make robots that are smarter and can work more autonomously, but robots that can take over the world?! Not quite.

THE FUTURE OF ROBOTS

Many scientists believe that the future of robotics is collaboration or, in other words, teamwork to make the dream work.

As we've seen, robots have already been helping us in our homes, in our hospitals, in factories, in space, and at the bottom of the ocean for years and years, so why shouldn't they carry on helping us?

These scientists believe in a future where humans and robots work together to create a better planet. When humans work together, they can achieve incredible things. Why can't the same be true of working with robots?

COBOTS

Rather than being locked away or working on their own, collaborative robots, or cobots, work right alongside humans. They don't replace us; they work with us! In the future, we might find more cobots in places we wouldn't usually expect them to be. Who knows, maybe one day they'll be driving our school buses, or working in our restaurants. Maybe they'll even be our friends!

WORD BLOCKS:

Humans are very good at learning things. We can use what we learn to solve problems. **This is called intelligence.**

Scientists are building machines and robots that can learn and deal with new situations. **This is called artificial intelligence.**

When a robot uses artificial intelligence (AI), we might say it's "smart".

For years and years, scientists have been trying to build machines that are as "smart" as humans.

THE TURING TEST

In 1950, a British mathematician called Alan Turing came up with a test to decide whether a computer is really intelligent or not. In the Turing test, a human judge would ask a question using a computer. A person and a computer would then answer the question at the same time. The judge would then try to tell which answer came from the computer and which came from the person. If the judge can't tell the difference, the computer must be intelligent!

FINDINGS/PROBLEMS:

So far, no computer has actually been able to pass this test. In fact, no computer has come close to passing it!

Computers can only use logic and facts to figure out problems, but humans use lots of other things, like their emotions and imagination.

Just because computers aren't yet as clever or as imaginative as humans are, this doesn't mean AI isn't already revolutionizing robotics. Lots of automated robots use AI and machine learning to help them work without humans and make decisions on their own. As scientists work to make AI better and better, robots will become more automated and more independent.

As robots can do more and more things on their own, our lives might start to look very different!

We know that robots can play chess, and we've seen that they can even play table tennis, but what about other sports and games? What about... soccer?

ROBOCUP

RoboCup is an annual international robotics competition that was started in 1996 by a group of university professors and is now the World Cup of robot soccer. Teams of soccer-playing robots from around the world that can run, kick, tackle, pass, and shoot, play soccer games against each other to be crowned the winner! RoboCup's goal is for a team of fully autonomous humanoid robot soccer players to beat the most recent winner of the FIFA World Cup in a game of soccer by the middle of the 21st century.

Sound ambitious? Good, that's the point! The people behind RoboCup want to inspire teams of scientists to test the limits of AI and robotics and to design and build amazing new autonomous machines.

If soccer's not your thing, how about racing? Not running racing – we're talking car racing, drone racing, and buggy racing. Racing with a need for speed.

ROBOT RACING

The Abu Dhabi Autonomous Racing League (A2RL) plans to have all of the speed that you'd expect from ordinary car racing, but with none of the drivers!

A2RL are on a mission to find out whether an autonomous car could ever drive faster than a human around a track. These robot cars use cameras, radar, and LiDAR technology to race. They use AI to know how hot the tires and brakes are, just like a human driver does, and to know when to steer, accelerate, shift gears, and brake.

The first ever A2RL autonomous car race was held in 2024. Autonomous car racing is still very new, so it can only get bigger, better, and faster in the future. Maybe one day we'll even be watching robot sports more than human ones!

It might be easy to imagine that nature and robotics are two very different worlds. How could they ever be important to each other?

We know that scientists are using robotics to save the planet, and roboticists are sometimes inspired by nature to create robots that look or act like animals. Bio-inspired robots are nothing new, but have you ever thought that robots that look like plants could be the future of planet-saving tech?

ROBOTIC FLOWERS

In 2003, scientists at MIT created the Cyberflora project, a mechanical flower garden made up of four types of robotic flowers. These robots look like flowers but act like animals! They are packed with sensors that can recognize light and touch and can react to the things happening around them.

POSSIBLE USES

Unfortunately, these robo-flowers didn't end up in the wild, but this kind of technology could be used to help our leafy friends in the future.

If robotic plants are planted alongside real plants, they could blend in like super-secret robot-spies. These undercover agents could be used to help monitor the temperature, humidity, light, or air quality of a space, all without anyone even knowing they're there! They could also help us create the best conditions for real plants to grow, which is very helpful of them indeed.

FUN FACT: SUPERTREES!

If you needed proof of how well technology and nature can work together, just take a look at the human-made mechanical forest of the Gardens by the Bay in Singapore. These 18 supertrees are made up of strong, steel frames, tropical flowers, and climbing ferns, and they work as vertical gardens. They collect rainwater that helps to water the conservatories below them, and their solar panels help to light up the forest.

These supertrees don't use robotics or AI, but just imagine what could be possible if they did!

If you've been paying attention, you'll know that when a robot is designed to look or act like something from nature, it's called biomimicry.

ROBOROYALE

RoboRoyale is a collaborative project between universities from around the world. The scientists who are working on this project are making use of biomimicry, microrobotics, and AI to create tiny, little robobees that could one day help real bees everywhere.

Unlike real bees, and unlike the other bee-bots, these little robots aren't interested in collecting nectar or in pollinating flowers, and they're not interested in the rest of their colony at all. In fact, you can barely even call them bees!

These robotic bees have been designed for one job and one job only: to look after the queen honeybee. Think of them like members of the queen's own royal court!

The plan is to send 6 to 8 of these robotic bees into the hive where they will be fitted with tiny cameras to analyze the queen bee and keep a camera-eye on how she behaves. These robots can groom the queen honeybee and feed her the right foods at the right time. Hopefully then, because these robots will be looking after the queen bee so well, she will start to lay more eggs. More eggs = more bees, and more bees = more pollination. And more pollination = more food for us hungry humans!

These robots aren't designed to replace real bees. Scientists want them to work alongside real bees, rather than replace them. By using biomimicry to create robots that fit into nature and fit into our lives, we will make big changes, all by taking care of one tiny queen bee!

At the moment, these robotic bees have to be controlled, but the goal is for them to be fully autonomous, so they can get to work without any help from humans. What busy little bees!

What do you think the greatest invention ever was? Maybe cars, or phones, or video game consoles? Well, think about this – maybe the greatest invention is plumbing, or in other words, water being piped in and out of your home. Think about it, without plumbing you wouldn't be able to drink water from the faucet... or flush the toilet. Ew!

So, it is safe to say plumbing is pretty important. But there's a big problem. All those pipes that carry water around a town or city are buried underground. And what happens if something goes wrong with a pipe? Most of the time, people have to dig up the road and look for problem. This is annoying for everyone, and it costs a lot of money.

However, four universities in the UK have been coming up with an idea – pipebots!

PIPEBOTS

These are tiny robots that can travel through pipes underground to find and fix leaks and damage.

Pipebots are 20 millimeters (0.79 inches) wide. They are built with sensors, cameras for eyes, and even a tail to help them swim if needed. They also use microphones to listen to the pipes, looking for small cracks that could turn into leaks one day.

It is hoped that groups of pipebots will work together to scan the network of underground pipes. These robots will be able to travel to places underground that humans can't get to.

Aside from saving money, pipebots will also help the environment. Wasting water is not good for our planet, so leaky pipes are bad news. Pipebots are good for humans and good for Earth.

These little robots are still being tested, but in the future they might be working hard in cities all around the world.

Would you eat at a robot restaurant? In the future, this might be a choice you have to make.

There are already a few robot restaurants in the world today. Many places already have touch-screen machines that can take your order. Some restaurants use conveyor belts to bring food to tables.

Robot chefs already exist, too. These machines can cook all sorts of food, from salads, to pasta, and burgers. They can make meals in just a few minutes. Now that is REAL fast food.

At the moment, robots in restaurants still need help from humans. While robots do a lot of the work, they still need people to help them prepare ingredients, talk to customers, or do other important jobs. Some robot waiters have even been fired for not being good enough!

Burgers and fries are pretty cheap, but you know what isn't cheap? Robots. This is partly why there aren't robot restaurants everywhere – the restaurants can't afford all these futuristic cooks and waiters. But in the future, as robots become cheaper, this might all change. And there are lots of reasons to get robots into the kitchens.

Robots do not get sick, and they do not need to be paid like humans. They don't need breaks, and they can often do a job quicker than humans. This could save restaurants a lot of money in the future.

When a robot does a job, it does it the same way every time. That means it can cook a tasty burger in the same way, forever. Unlimited tasty burgers! Yay!

THE ROBOT REVOLUTION IS COMING...

and it might not be too long before they are everywhere, living side by side with humans. But what happens if robots get smarter and more powerful than humans? Do we need any rules to make sure nothing goes wrong?

A man called Isaac Asimov thought we needed rules. Asimov wrote stories about robots, and then came up with three rules he thought were important for the future of robotics.

RULE 1

A robot must never injure a human being.

RULE 2

A robot must always follow orders given by a human (except if the order is to hurt another human, because that would break Rule 1).

RULE 3

A robot must protect itself, as long as it doesn't cause them to break Rule 1 or Rule 2.

But robots are becoming smarter and smarter. What about the super-intelligent humanoid robots of the future – should they be treated in the same way that we treat robot arms or drones? Or should they be treated like people?

Do you remember reading about Sophia in earlier? Sophia is an intelligent robot that can understand human speech. In 2017, the country of Saudi Arabia gave Sophia a passport and made her a citizen of that country. And she is the first non-human to own a credit card. Sophia is becoming more and more like a person every day.

Maybe it is time to talk about

ROBOT RIGHTS.

Humans have rights. Rights are like a set of rules for how people should be treated in a fair way. For example, you have the right to go to school, and you have the right to clothes and food.

So, the big question is this: should robots have rights?

What rights would you give the intelligent robots of the future?

So, robots are cool, robots are important, and robots are saving the world. But what next? How can we carry on building robots for good?

There are so many more robots to create and build, and you could be the brains behind some of the next world-changing robotic inventions that help us and our planet!

Inventing robots is all about intelligence, innovation, and creativity. and a whole load of science, of course!

There are some international robotics competitions that have been set up especially to inspire the next generation of roboticists. Could this be you?!

GLOBAL ROBOTIC GAMES

This competition was started in Singapore and encourages students to work as part of a team to design, program, and operate new robots. In 2024, the theme was H2O Heroes. Students were encouraged to focus on water sustainability, and how we can use robots to protect water resources and make sure everyone has access to clean and safe drinking water.

WORLD ROBOT OLYMPIAD

The World Robot Olympiad was started by China, Japan, Singapore, and Korea, and the first international final was held in Singapore. Tournaments are now organized in over 95 countries all over the world to inspire budding teenage roboticists to create the robots of the future.

FIRST ROBOTICS COMPETITION

FIRST stands for For Inspiration and Recognition of Science and Technology, and its mission is to prepare young people for the future through inclusive and team-based robotics programs. FIRST's international high school robotics competitions are like games, and they can involve robots kicking balls into goals or hanging from bars. The competitions are all about "coopertition". This means that teams help and cooperate with each other, even when they're competing against each other! After all, we can only change the world if we work together, and humanity only wins if we all win.

Robots are the future, but so are you! Robots can only change the world if we create them. **Are you ready to start building?**

TOMORROW'S WORLD

Tomorrow's World is an exciting series that takes readers on an unforgettable journey into the core of the coolest sciences our world has **EVER** seen.

From the wonders of space and the depths of the oceans to the exciting possibilities of AI and the risks of an asteroid hitting Earth (gulp), this series is overflowing with fascinating facts and comic-style illustrations, showing how scientists around the world are constantly shaping (and saving) our future.

Written by renowned authors and reviewed by specialists in the field, each book is a perfect blend of fun, adventure, and of course, a fart joke or two.

This series inspires young readers to not just dream big, but to dream of tomorrow. **The future of science begins here!**

If you enjoyed this book, check out some of the other titles in the series: